Dear Warren —
Enjoy! fondly Chula

I0607320

Sea of Japan

◊ OTOKOYAMA

**Hokkaido**
Sapporo ○
30
18,000

◊ KIKUHIME
◊ FUKUMASAMUNE
◊ ARAMASA
◊ HIRA IZUMI
◊ HATSUMAGO
◊ TATEYAMA
◊ ŌYAMA
◊ KOSHINOKAMBAI
⚑ CHIYODA
◊ KUSUDAMA
◊ KOSHINO-HOMARE

AOMORI
62
13,000
Aomori ○

◊ MOMOKAWA

AKITA
62
42,000
Akita ○

Morioka ○
35
15,000
IWATE

Sado Island

YAMAGATA
41
25,000
Yamagata ○

56
11,000

◊ ICHINOKURA

MIYAGI

Niigata ○
113
43,000

○ Niigata

◊ URAKASUMI

Sendai ○

53
17,000
IKAWA
nazawa
34
13,000
Toyama ○
TOYAMA

NIIGATA

Fukushima ○
113
50,000

◊ TARUHEI

Nagano ○

Pacific Ocean

GIFU
77
,000

111
35,000
NAGANO

GUMMA
48
9,000
Maebashi ○

FUKUSHIMA

◊ EISEN

**Honshu**

TOCHIGI
54
13,000
Utsunomiya ○

Kōfu ○
29
6,000
YAMANASHI

SAITAMA
67
25,000
Urawa ○

IBARAKI
73
18,000
Mito ○

◊ SHIKIZAKURA

SHIZUOKA
55
,000
Shizuoka ○

TOKYO
KANAGAWA
23
4,000

18
5,000
Tokyo ○
Chiba ○
Yokohama ○

◊ HITORIMUSUME

CHIBA
51
15,000

◊ KIDOIZUMI
◊ IWANOI

⚑ GENJI

◊ MASUMI

◊ WAKATAKE ONIKOROSHI

◊ NANAWARAI

NATIONAL TOTAL   2,772 / 1,191,000

30 / 18,000 ⟶  number of makers / production by prefecture (kiloliters)

◊ IWANOI ⟶ local saké (*jizake*)
⚑ GENJI ⟶ export saké

- - - - -  Route of saké cargo ships (*taru kaisen*) to Edo

═══════  Tōkaidō: inland route to Edo

X'mas "86"

# SAKÉ
## A Drinker's Guide

Hiroshi Kondō
with a Foreword by
**George Plimpton**

KODANSHA INTERNATIONAL LTD.
Tokyo, New York and San Francisco

# CONTENTS

JAPANESE WORDS: Japanese words in this book, in both italics and roman letters, should in all cases be pronounced as they are written. Every syllable is voiced, including a final "e" that would normally be unvoiced in English (only the word "saké" in roman letters has been given an accent for clarity; the accent is dropped when the word appears in italics as part of a Japanese phrase). Vowels that appear with a macron, or "long sign" (ō and ū), are elongated when spoken (*oo* as in "boat," *uu* as in "moon"). Sometimes consonants and vowels at the beginnings or ends of words undergo sound modification when used in compound constructions: "saké," for example, can become either *saka-* or *-zake*. Note that brewers are not systematic about how they romanize the Japanese names of their products. Except where it would be confusing, this text follows the makers' usages.

Names of premodern historical figures are, according to accepted convention, given family name first, while names of modern-day Japanese (post-1868) are given in Western style, personal name first.

MEASUREMENTS: Linear and volume measurements are given here in the metric system: 1 kilometer is a bit more than half a mile, 1 liter is a bit more than a quart, 1 kilogram is a bit more than 2 pounds, and so on. Temperatures are given in both centigrade (C) and fahrenheit (F). In recipes intended for home use, weight measurements are given in grams and ounces, while liquid and volume measures are given in units familiar to all American kitchens—cups, teaspoons, tablespoons.

Distributed in the United States by Kodansha International/USA Ltd., through Harper & Row, Publishers, Inc., 10 East 53rd Street, New York, New York 10022. Published by Kodansha International Ltd., 12-21, Otowa 2-chome, Bunkyo-ku, Tokyo 112 and Kodansha International/USA Ltd., with offices at 10 East 53rd Street, New York, New York 10022 and at The Hearst Building, 5 Third Street, Suite 430, San Francisco, California 94103.

**Library of Congress Cataloging in Publication Data**

Kondō, Hiroshi, 1924–
    Saké: a drinker's guide.

    Includes index.
    1. Rice wines. I. Title.
TP579.K6    1984        641.2'2        83-48880
ISBN 0-87011-653-3 (U.S.)
ISBN4-7700-1153-9 (in Japan)

# *Foreword*

Dining in a Japanese restaurant I am often reminded of a *New Yorker* cartoon in which the husband, about to order from an extensive menu, is shown leaning across the table to ask his wife: "Which is it I can't abide—sushi or sashimi?"

No wonder, faced as this good gentleman is with the plethora and variety of Japanese fare. There is, however, one item listed on the menu about which he would have few doubts . . . and that is saké and the pleasures it affords. One of its particular delights, of course, is that it comes to the table in its fragile porcelain bottle heated; one can remember only mulled wine, the hot toddy, and Irish coffee as equivalently warmed drinks from the Western culture, and these are served mainly to ward off the chills of winter. The great property of saké, at least for the non-purist like myself, is that it provides the curious, almost sensual satisfaction that is derived from the warmth of the drink against the palate.

I have described myself as a "non-purist" because I have discovered in my reading of this volume that the professional tasting of saké should be done at room temperature, specifically 64–68 degrees fahrenheit. Apparently, heat destroys the subtleties of taste. I was not aware of that, nor that saké enjoys as complex and studied a tradition of being judged for its qualities as wine. I am not alone in my ignorance. I was once told by the Japanese-American bartender of the excellent Japanese restaurant in New York's Hotel Woodward that there is no difference between the tastes of sakés produced in California and those from Japan. In fact, he stated bluntly that it was impossible to tell *any* sakés apart. As illustration, he added that it was no more possible to distinguish one saké from another than it was to tell the difference between ginger ale and Coca-Cola! I should have realized from his startling analogy that I had been talking with a man possessed of astonishingly feeble taste buds. Indeed, it turns out that in the lexicon of saké tasting there are ninety-odd terms to describe the qualities of the drink. Curiously, these are more derogatory than salutary terms. Among the former (in English) are "cloying," "garrulous," "thick," and "ill-bred." I intend to tell my friend, the bartender, the next time I visit the Hotel Woodward, and perhaps we will do some testing to see which words of those ninety-odd descriptions apply. I am especially hopeful of finding a saké that would be specified as "garrulous." It would be worth tasting even if it outraged (which it probably would) the taste buds.

To help us in our research (though I would continually have grave doubts about my companion's ability to judge that he even had any liquid in his mouth), there is a fascinating chapter on saké tasting in this volume. It states that the walls of the tasting room should be a "light cream color" (with north-facing windows to provide the best natural light), that there is a best time of the day to taste (between ten and eleven)—neither of these requirements are applicable to the bar of the Hotel Woodward's Japanese restaurant, gloomy and closed until noon—and that one should avoid wearing colognes or, God forbid, a hair spray on the day of a tasting. The author warns: "Conversations not having to do with saké should be carried on away from the tasting area."

I have wondered why often the delicate saké cups that arrive at one's table in restaurants have two concentric blue circles in the bottom. Now I know. They are patterned after tasting cups, what are called "snake's eye" cups. The color of a saké is as important a consideration as its taste and bouquet (what is referred to rather pungently in this volume as "smell"); the snake-eye pattern of blue is used as a backdrop against which to judge the relative transparencies of the sakés.

No less interesting is the material in this volume on the history of saké. It is unlikely that I will ever ask for saké in the future without recalling that first sakés were produced from rice chewed by villagers and spat into a large wooden tub. An early experimenter had discovered that an element in saliva was instrumental in the fermentation process. Chewing to produce an alcoholic beverage is not an unknown practice in other cultures. The Masato Indians of Peru chew yucca plants to produce a kind of beer. But the Japanese have a particularly memorable tradition. The best of their ancient sakés were those prepared by "young virgins"—the brand produced called *bijinshu*—the "beautiful woman saké." This technique was reputedly practiced until recent times in a few Ainu villages in Hokkaido and in the backcountry of Okinawa. Splendid!—a far more appealing method to conjure, it can be said, than the thought of French peasants stomping their bare feet in a vat of grapes!

A term in this book about the taste of a good saké sticks in the mind. It is that a fine saké "has a tail"—a translation of the tasting terms *shiripin* and *pin*. That is to say, if the saké has a lingering pleasant aftertaste that is hard to forget one has discovered that it "has a tail." It is hard to think of a more pleasing search . . . or one with such splendid rewards. I imagine myself in the gloom of the Hotel Woodward or wherever, calling out *Kore da!*—the Japanese equivalent of "Eureka! I have discovered a saké with a tail!"

*New York City, 1984*                                          GEORGE PLIMPTON

# PART 1

# Saké:
# Japan's Good Drink

Large vat, probably used in the manufacture of saké
sometime around the 6th to 8th century. Isonokami
Shrine, Nara.

Casks of saké given as offerings to Ōmi Shrine, Shiga
Prefecture.

What a saké banquet must have looked like at the Heian court in the 11th century. The courtier in the center is holding a small saké cup. (*Murasaki Shikibu Nikki Ekotoba*, 13th century.)

Saké drinking at the home of a samurai. Saké is first poured into a cask and then brought into the banquet room by servants. (*Shuhan-ron*, Muromachi period.)

Detail of folding screen showing a party for samurai at a house of courtesans in about the mid-1600s. The bald-headed guest is holding a large saké cup in his right hand. (*Yūraku-zu Byōbu*, Edo period.)

An early Edo-period public drinking house. The customer at right with the peaked headcovering is a samurai. Townsmen are in various degrees of intoxication. The man at left is drawing saké from a cask into a small wooden container called a *masu*. (*Kinsei Shokunin-zukushi Ekotoba*, by Kuwakata Keisai, Edo period.)

A government reception banquet for Dutch merchants in Nagasaki. A display of sliced raw fish is on the stand at left. At right, a woman dances. (*Kagetsu Ranjin Yūkyō-zu*, late Edo period.)

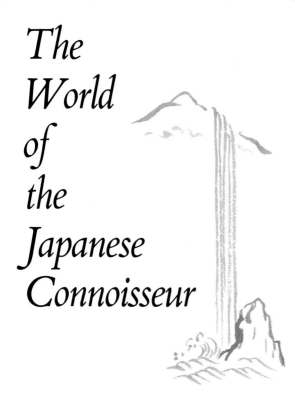

# The World of the Japanese Connoisseur

## The Drink of the Gods

The *Kojiki*, one of Japan's oldest historical chronicles, traces the origin of saké to the age of the gods. Susanoonomikoto, brother of the sun goddess Amaterasu, is said to have saved Princess Kushinada from the Great Serpent of Yamata Lake by brewing eight huge vats of saké, enticing the Great Serpent to drink, and then slaying him with a magical sword. According to some saké connoisseurs, especially those who have been imbibing freely, Susanoonomikoto's brewing techniques were adopted by early Japanese people and have been passed down intact to the present day. More likely, sophisticated brewing methods started coming to Japan from China in about the 7th century, probably by two routes: one directly from the southeastern provinces, and the other by way of Korea. The *Kojiki* itself records how a foreign brewmaster by the name of Susukori came to Japan as early as the 3rd century A.D. and brewed rice wine for the emperor Ōjin.

The Japanese, however, were drinking saké even before their first contact with China. Local histories written during the Nara period (710–94) suggest that the first saké in Japan was called *kuchikami no sake*, or "chewing-in-the-mouth saké." As its unsavory name suggests, this saké was made by chewing rice, chestnuts, or millet and then spitting the

wad into a large wooden tub, where it was allowed to brew for several days. We know today that enzymes contained in saliva will convert starch into glucose, which will in turn be converted into alcohol as airborne yeast grow on the mash.

The brewing of this most ancient of sakés was one of the rituals performed during Shinto religious festivals. There were many local variations. In some areas, the head of the village would lead all the members of the village in performing the ceremony of chewing the rice and spitting it into a vessel. In one of the most common forms of the ritual, said to have been practiced until recent times in some Ainu villages in Hokkaido and in rural areas of Okinawa, only young virgins were allowed to chew the rice. These virgins were considered mediums of the gods, and the saké they produced was called *bijinshu*, or "beautiful woman saké."

Aside from the imported brewing techniques, the most significant advances toward producing a unique Japanese saké seem to have been made by accident. *Harima Fudoki*, one of the Nara-period local histories, relates how a cask of steamed rice was once accidentally left uncovered. The owner found to his horror that the rice had molded. Negligent man that he had already proven himself to be, he failed to dispose of it. Several days later, he discovered that the cask of spoiled rice had been transformed into a cask of delicious saké. Similar incidents must have occurred in other places, for the ancients soon learned that it was the mold that caused this wonderful transformation, and that part of the rice infected by this mold, which they called *kamutachi*, could be saved to start a new batch of saké. This *kamutachi*, which the ancients thought was produced when the gods partook of the rice, corresponds to what is now called *kōji* (*Aspergillum oryzae*), and it is the use of this mold that makes saké brewing so special, as we shall see in a later section.

Pitcher with straw for drinking diluted saké mash, used from about the 5th century.

Pincer-chopsticks for "eating" saké, used from about the 6th century.

At the Asakusa Sanja Festival in Tokyo, brawny young men filled with enthusiasm—and saké—shoulder a portable shrine. Chanting and heaving, they parade it through the streets to bestow the blessings of the local god on the neighborhood. Thousands of festivals similar to this one take place each year throughout Japan. They have evolved from the earliest celebrations of a rice-growing culture and are sometimes frightening displays of raw, intoxicating forces.

Saké was still a far cry from what we drink today. The ancients had not yet discovered yeast, and their saké contained very little alcohol. Moreover, because very little water was used in the brewing, saké was more a lightly fermented mixture of rice and kōji rice that had the consistency of oatmeal. Indeed, in the language of this period, you did not "drink" saké, you "ate" it. The fermented mash was heaped into a shallow bowl and eaten with a pair of chopsticks joined at the top and resembling pincers. Among the extant saké implements from this period are broad-mouthed pitchers in which the mash was mixed with water and drunk through an earthenware straw.

The most important aspect of drinking saké in this period, and one that still survives today, was its profound social and religious significance. In early Japan, societies were communal and agricultural, highly dependent on close-knit cooperation among families and on natural climatic conditions. As in the ritual of *kuchikami no sake*, making and drinking saké in a group served to consecrate the fictive kinship relationships that held the community together. Offering saké to the gods would calm their violent spirits and tempt them to descend and give benefits to the realm of human beings. At the same time, by partaking of this marvelous beverage, human beings could assume godlike qualities.

The power of the gods was needed in the first place of course to transform the rice, kōji rice, and water into saké. While the ceremonial drinking was performed in the presence of all the gods, a few gods were believed to take a personal interest in the magical brewing process. Three of the most famous, Ōyamatsumi no kami, Konohanasakuya-hime, and Sukunahikona no mikoto, are today enshrined in such well-known Shinto shrines as the Ōmiwa Shrine in Nara and the shrines of Matsuo and Umemiya in Kyoto. Saké's early connection with the gods makes it today the ritual drink of choice at almost all traditional ceremonies and celebrations. It is an essential part of wedding feasts, shrine festivals, and building dedications, bestowing a divinely good feeling on humans who raise their cups in honor and appreciation.

## Classical Japan and the Ideal of Fūryū

In the late Nara period and in the Heian period (794–1185), when the court of the emperor was located in Kyoto, the introduction of T'ang-dynasty culture from China revolutionized Japanese society. Japanese emissaries to China returned with news of Confucianism, Buddhism, Chinese political institutions, and the poetry and prose of China's most illustrious period, the High T'ang. While Confucian concepts of government discouraged frivolity of any kind, Chinese literature, Taoism, and Buddhism depicted a completely different world, in which a man's private life was separate from his rigidly defined public life. The private life so depicted was one of intense passions, a love of wine, music, poetry, and beautiful women: in short, the world of connoisseurship that the Japanese called *fūryū*, a term literally meaning "the flow of the wind." *Fūryū*—"taste," "elegance," "wit"—as a borrowed concept would dominate Japanese notions of pleasure for centuries.

It was at this time that the rituals of drinking saké took on a more social aspect. The staid T'ang ideals of elegance prescribed that public occasions in which the gods were present (the emperor was considered a descendant of the sun goddess) would be ceremonial and formal. Chinese was even adopted as the official language at court. But the *fūryū* ideal led to the parallel development of a richly aesthetic and lyrical private culture where one could imbibe at leisure with friends. Here the language spoken was Japanese, and it has been passed down to us in the diaries and novels of beautiful women who were at the center of the constantly bubbling broth of court intrigues and innuendo—and romance.

Pointing up the differences between these two worlds are the Fujiwara brothers, Michinaga and Michitaka. Michinaga had established his family as preeminent in the Heian court. Michitaka established his reputation as a famous drinker. It was said of Michitaka that he was never without a flask of saké at hand; on one occasion, he became so intoxicated while riding from the court to his own mansion that he fell out of his carriage en route. We also have accounts of private imperial banquets in which certain court ladies were summoned from behind the standing screens that normally shielded them to serve saké with very little ceremony indeed. Murasaki Shikibu, the author of that revealing novel of court life, *The Tale of Genji*, complains in her diary of the debauchery that often accompanied these private banquets.

But while the Japanese are famous borrowers, they seldom leave what they have borrowed unchanged. This was true of the brewing techniques that were borrowed from China, and it was also true of *fūryū*. It was during the Heian period that flower-viewing, moon-viewing, and many other Chinese occasions for drinking were adapted to Japanese sensibilities, becoming much more closely related to ancient beliefs connected with the indigenous animist faith of Shinto than to ideas imported from China. The Japanese believed that

The "Well of the Gods" at Matsuo Shrine, Kyoto. Saké made from water drawn here is said to have special protective properties.

the cherry blossoms possessed an innate vitality that would infect those who gathered beneath them to drink and recite poetry. This idea partakes of ancient Japanese ceremonial drunkfests. The imported Buddhism and Confucianism did not prevent such beliefs from finding their full expression in Heian times. Nor do westernization and modern cynicism interfere with the pleasure that Japanese experience today when they make excursions to places famous for their cherry blossoms to drink saké and enjoy the beauty of spring.

The affluent society of the Heian court contributed a great deal to the development of saké-brewing techniques. Professor Kin'ichirō Sakaguchi, the father of modern academic studies on the history of saké, refers to this period as the "age of the court." While the common people continued to enjoy the crude saké prepared for festivals and other ritual events, the court established its own saké brewery and commissioned an independent class of artisans to produce the many types of saké it required for presentation to the gods, for their own consumption, and for their retainers. These artisans came from families that specialized in different stages of brewing. Interestingly enough, considering the tradition of "beautiful woman saké," women seem to have played the principal ceremonial role in saké production. The brewery was within the palace compound itself, and produced "white saké," no

doubt a more refined, liquid version of the commoners' saké, as well as "black saké," which was flavored with the ashes of aromatic wood, "chrysanthemum saké," and many other varieties.

Unfortunately, Confucian ideals of scholarship did not encourage interest in anything so mundane as a manufacturing process, so contemporary records describing the details of saké brewing do not exist. But it is clear that the artisans in the court brewery had a thorough knowledge of Chinese techniques. For example, the *Engi Shiki*, a code promulgated in 905 to stipulate procedures and forms to be followed at court, indicates that white saké and the other sakés designated for consumption by the gods and people of noble birth were clarified sakés. That is, they were obtained by dipping out the saké at the very top of a brewing vat after the mash had settled, or by filling cloth sacks with the fermented mash and allowing the saké to filter through. Both were Chinese techniques, the latter being identical to the method still employed today in traditional Japanese breweries. The practice of drinking saké warm during the cold months of the year also originated in the Heian period, probably under the influence of Chinese models. Where, however, the Chinese-type saké, *lao shou*, used a glutenous rice and was brewed in sealed containers, the Japanese used a less-glutenous rice and left the mash to ferment in open-top casks. The Japanese would not learn to use polished white rice until much later.

It is difficult to convey the extent to which drinking and all its attendant pleasures were developed during the Heian period. The literature of the period provides many examples of how the concept of *fūryū* in the Heian court was translated into an expansive set of behaviors and perceptions of beauty, taste, and elegance that are still revered by modern Japanese. *The Tale of Genji* reveals the extent to which the court aesthetic shaped saké culture, adding to the purely native celebrant strain a layer of careful, cultivated, mannered enjoyment that from today's perspective may seem abnormally precious and effete. The *Engi Shiki* provides a wealth of information concerning the various banquets and ceremonies performed at court, and also tells us that, besides the brewery directly connected to the court, 180 other breweries existed in Kyoto at this time.

Unfortunately, the early literature provides only tantalizing glimpses of the way saké was enjoyed by the common people. Probably they got drunk. We know from a proclamation issued in 646 that the court found it necessary to ban excessive consumption of saké by lower-ranking people, and we know from the fact that these proclamations were issued repeatedly during the succeeding centuries that they were generally ignored.

What is perhaps most interesting in the *Engi Shiki* is that it reveals an aspect of formal drinking in Japan that still survives and is completely foreign to modern Western concepts of drinking as a social pastime. This aspect might be compared to the tea ceremony in Japan, but it could also be compared to the formal banquets in medieval Europe, or perhaps ancient Egypt. The idea of everyone drinking together at the same time simply did not exist in classical Japan (or, for that matter, in medieval Japan). The host of the banquet, who in extant records is usually an emperor, commanded elegantly attired servants to pour saké into a large shallow bowl. He imbibed first and then passed the bowl on to the highest-ranking guest. The bowl continued to pass around the table until the courtier of lowest rank had had his turn. This ritual was performed three times. At the point the formal banquet was over, the informal ("hidden from the gods") banquet could begin. These "hidden" banquets were quite unrestrained. The same sort of formal toasting continued, but music and entertainment began after the second round, and in the midst of all this ritual there was a good deal of imbibing indeed as courtiers waited their turn for the imperial cup.

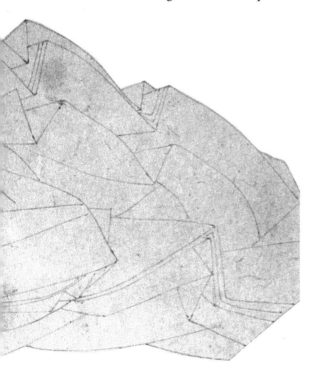

Detail from a Kamakura-period scroll painting based on *The Pillow Book of Sei Shōnagon*, a lady's miscellaneous observations on life and the court in Heian times. The woman here is shown playing a lutelike *biwa*.

THE LADIES-IN-WAITING RUSTLED THEIR ROBES BEHIND THE SCREEN AT THE SOUTHERN PORCH AND CAME OUT. THERE WERE GREAT NUMBERS OF COURTIERS SITTING IN THE CORRIDOR AND ON THE BRIDGE OVER THE GARDEN. HIS MAJESTY SUMMONED THE OFFICIALS OF CEREMONIAL AND BADE THEM BRING FRUIT, SAKÉ, AND FOOD, SAYING, "MAKE EVERYONE DRUNK." AND TRULY THE COURTIERS GOT DRUNK. THEY EXCHANGED ELEGANT WORDS WITH THE LADIES BEHIND THE SCREEN, AND EVERYONE FOUND EACH OTHER QUITE FASCINATING.
—from *The Pillow Book of Sei Shōnagon*

Warrior deity at entry to the temple Tōdaiji, Nara, showing the violent Kamakura style. Ca. 1200.

## The Middle Ages

The imperial court in Kyoto came to rely increasingly on local warriors to enforce central decisions, and as the military power of these warriors increased so did their ambitions. The most prominent of the warrior families, the Taira and the Minamoto, were able to exploit the factional squabbles within the imperial family both to enhance their power at court and to justify their own positions in the frequent skirmishes between them. This situation climaxed in the year 1179, when Taira Kiyomori seized control of the government in Kyoto on the pretext that he was acting on behalf of "imperial authority."

This sparked the legendary Gempei War, which raged for five years from 1180 to 1185 and provided much of the material for medieval Japanese literature. Minamoto Yoritomo emerged victorious and established the first Japanese shogunate at Kamakura, several hundred kilometers to the east. While the court continued to play a central role in cultural affairs (Kyoto was still the "capital"), the Kamakura warriors developed new political, legal, and economic institutions that revolutionized society. The role of saké in this new medieval age was also transformed.

Professor Sakaguchi calls this period in the history of saké the "age of temples and shrines." With the advent of a stable currency, a new commercial economy developed. Saké brewing was one of the first industries that arose to supply this market. Descendants of the families that had run the saké brewery of the court now sought permission from the new government to establish themselves as independent brewers, or formed guilds, associating themselves with powerful temples and shrines and going into business under their protection. Many temples and shrines had already established brewing operations during the Nara period, taking advantage of their extensive holdings of rice lands and well-organized work forces of monks. In the middle ages these religious institutions expanded their activities further. Saké retailers joined other merchants in the large markets that were held periodically at the gates of temples and shrines, and public drinking establishments appeared in Kamakura and the capital.

The years of hard fighting and rugged living had produced a warrior code of behavior that emphasized courage, manliness, and austerity. The rough, provincial warriors of the new ruling class were the exact opposites of the effete court nobility. Yoritomo even forbade social contacts between members of the military class and the nobility, believing with good reason that it was their long years at court which had weakened the leaders of the defeated Taira clan. Less than ten years after Yoritomo's death in 1199, however, the favorites of the new shogun, Sanetomo, were not stern warriors but elegant Kyoto courtiers, and Sanetomo's favorite pastime was Japanese poetry.

Even without this infusion of courtly tastes, which with the court's loss of power had turned increasingly to wine, women, and song, the members of the warrior class were no strangers to the attractions of saké. In 1252, when the imperial prince Munetaka was installed as shogun, the regent Hōjō Tokiyori was forced to issue sumptuary laws limiting the amount of saké produced in Kamakura to 1 jar for each household, and the proclamation deplores the fact that there were more than 37,000 jars of saké in the city. More and more, the scions of the great warrior families looked to Kyoto for their standards of taste and behavior, and were infected by the ideals of *fūryū*.

In 1334, the Kamakura period came to an end when an imperial succession dispute sparked a civil war that would last for more than fifty years until the consolidation of the Ashikaga shogunate in 1392. During the subsequent Muromachi period (1392–1573), which derives its name from the district in Kyoto where the shogunate made its headquarters, rapid advances were made both in the brewing of saké and the culture that surrounded it.

The leaders of the Ashikaga family made no pretense of being rough provincial warriors. Ashikaga Yoshimitsu, who already held effective control over the government by 1368, is famous in Japanese history as much for his ostentation and the lavish culture of which he was the center as for his military and political prowess. Yoshimitsu was a true Kyoto man, and quite at ease among courtiers.

The elite of the warrior class did, however, attempt to distinguish their own culture from that of the court. An enormous expansion of trade with Sung China and Korea made available a wide range of luxury items. The ideals of *fūryū* espoused by the military class in opposition to the refined elegance of the court is perhaps best symbolized by the opulence of the Chinese fabrics, porcelain, and art objects they imported and by their extravagantly formal banquets.

Professor Sakaguchi calls this period the "age of independent brewers." There was a steady increase in internal trade during this period, and while

Chinese-style carved lacquer stand for tea bowl. Ca. 1430.

temples and shrines continued to play an important role, the commercialization of saké led to the rise of independent brewers throughout the country, many of whom were also wealthy and influential money exchangers. By the end of the 14th century, there were 342 brewers in Kyoto alone.

The competition between independent brewers and the guilds associated with temples, shrines, and official patrons led to rapid advances in brewing. Priests of the temple Shōrekiji in Nara developed a technique of brewing with a yeast starter mash. Guilds associated with the Kitano Shrine in Kyoto discovered a process of drying and preserving kōji spores, and began marketing various types of kōji for use in saké, miso (soybean paste), and soy sauce.

At least by this time connoisseurs were making distinctions between sakés. The best-known saké in the early 15th century was produced by an independent brewer named Chūkō Shirōzaemon, whose shop in the Gojō district of Kyoto was called Yanagi no Saké, or ''Willow Saké.'' Shogun Ashikaga Yoshimasa was inordinately fond of this saké, and arranged for the Chūkō family to pay its taxes in casks of it. Also famous during this period were Amanozaké, produced at the temple of Kongōji in Amano (modern Nagano City near Osaka), and Narazaké, produced at subtemples of Kōfukuji and Shōrekiji in Nara. Later, in the latter half of the 16th century, these temples developed *morohaku* sakés, or sakés for which all of the rice used in brewing was polished white rice. Polishing removed many of the proteins and minerals responsible for off-flavors and impurities in the final brew. At Kongōji today, one can still see the vats that were used in brewing and the stoneware casks in which the saké was stored.

The aristocracy and the military elite were not the only classes active in creating the new Muromachi culture. Foreign trade and the development of a commercial economy created a new class of wealthy merchants in Kyoto, as well as in new cities such as Sakai on the Inland Sea and Kanazawa on the west coast. These merchants were no less avid in their pursuit of *fūryū* than the military men, and became patrons of art, literature, crafts, and the Noh theater.

It is also in this period that we begin to see the emergence of a class of commoners—townsmen, itinerant monks, nuns, performers—that would later become the most vital force in Japanese culture. Especially in the world of wandering Zen monks do we see enacted a new brand of *fūryū*, bound neither by courtly concepts of elegance or the warrior class's elaborate decorum. These monks rejected both the honors offered by the court and the high offices offered by the Buddhist establishment. They lived among the common people and wrote about what they saw and heard. In his formal writings, the famous eccentric Ikkyū (1394–1484) lamented the popularity of brothels and drinking establishments in the capital, but it is clear from his more casual jottings that this monk found much to enjoy as a connoisseur.

Entertainment at a house of courtesans in about the mid-1600s. (*Yūraku-zu Byōbu*, Edo period.)

One cannot discuss saké and the way it was enjoyed at this time without reference to the tea ceremony. Tea was first introduced into Japan from China in the 8th century. In the 12th century, Japanese Zen monks reintroduced and began drinking tea to stay alert during their long hours of meditation. Tea drinking was also taken up in a more elaborate style by the Ashikaga shoguns and the Kyoto aristocracy. Zen anti-materialist ideals eventually fused with the courtly banqueting style to produce a formalized ritual of imbibing and eating in a contrived naturalistic setting of poverty and restraint.

Everything about the tea ceremony was fastidiously coordinated to produce tranquillity and to awaken the mind to beauty and to the profoundly simple truths of the world. The approach garden was made to resemble a mountain path. Inside the tea room, looking more like a farmer's hut and perhaps only 2 square meters in area, there would be a small floral display, a hanging scroll with a scene and poem appropriate to the season. The tea

AS I WAS LEAVING THE TEMPLE OF NYOIAN, I LEFT THIS FOR MASTER YŌSŌ:

I HAVE BEEN TEN DAYS IN THIS TEMPLE,
AND MY HEART IS RESTLESS,
THE SCARLET THREAD OF LUST AT MY FEET
HAS REACHED UP LONG.
IF SOME DAY YOU COME SEARCHING FOR ME,
I WILL BE IN A SHOP THAT SELLS FINE SEAFOOD, A GOOD
DRINKING PLACE, OR A BROTHEL.
—Ikkyū

utensils might be rough and irregular, embodying the qualities of their material and disavowing the human hand that had shaped them.

The tea aesthetic that developed at this time, particularly under the guidance of its greatest master, Sen no Rikyū (1520–91), was a powerful influence on the still-evolving blend of Japanese *fūryū*. Many kinds of saké cups, for example, had been employed during the period, including priceless

porcelain from Sung China and gorgeous lacquerwares produced in Japan. But by the beginning of the 17th century the highest esteem was paid to the coarser native pottery, which struck European observers like João Rodrigues as very strange. In *This Island of Japon*, Rodrigues, a Portuguese Jesuit, notes "the ordinary [saké] cups are painted with a very delicate lacquer, adorned with wonderfully and richly gilded flowers" while the festive or formal ones are merely made of baked clay, "in accordance with their ancient customs and ceremonies, when they could use other ware made of precious materials such as gold and silver."

Elaborate tea ceremonies were frequently preceded by a meal—called *kaiseki*—consisting of saké, of course, accompanied by tidbits of fish, fresh vegetables, pickles, sauces, and occasionally wild game, each tastefully arranged on its own small plate. The food was, in keeping with the goals of the ceremony, not only delicious but beautiful. This ideal of Japanese cuisine extended even to the most opulent banquets, where guests would be served more than fifty different foods on three to seven

decorative trays. Rodrigues and his contemporaries were the first foreigners to complain that Japanese cuisine is beautiful to look at but cold and insipid to the palate.

Japanese drinking customs followed the same pattern. Saké was never drunk alone but always accompanied by small servings of food called *sakana*;

Typical *kaiseki* meal served with tea ceremony: rice, miso soup, fish and vegetables.

Zen monks conducting a tea ceremony in a grass hut. (*Shunjū Shijo Yūraku-zu*, Muromachi period.)

perhaps the modern version of this ancient fare, which often includes cooked meats like beef and chicken, would be more to Rodrigues's liking.

The Muromachi period "officially" ends in 1573, when the warlord Oda Nobunaga ended yet another period of almost constant warfare by deposing the last Ashikaga shogun and establishing his own headquarters in Osaka. Nobunaga was assassinated in 1582 and was succeeded by his general Toyotomi Hideyoshi, who ruled supreme in Japan until his death in 1598. This was followed by more conspiracy and war that lasted until 1603, when Tokugawa Ieyasu founded a shogunate that would endure in peace until the Meiji Restoration of 1868, which marks the end of the medieval era and the beginning of modernization and westernization.

The *Taikōki*, a history of Hideyoshi's rise to power and his illustrious reign, contains a wealth of information concerning saké and the way it was consumed. In March of 1598, Hideyoshi staged the greatest cherry-blossom-viewing banquet in Japanese history, a truly elaborate affair that lasted several days with hundreds of guests and entertainments, picnicking, and much carousing. The sakés chosen for this occasion are described in some detail. Kikuzaké, or "chrysanthemum saké," was produced in the port city of Miyakoshi (present-day Kanazawa). The water used in brewing this saké was said to be drawn from the river running into the harbor on the morning of the day the chrysanthemum blossoms were at the peak of their beauty, just after they had dropped their morning dew into the current. Asajizaké was brought from the province of Higo in Kyushu, and Nerinukizaké

from the province of Chikuzen (Fukuoka Prefecture). Of course, the *morohaku* sakés from Nara and Amano were served, as were sakés from the large breweries that had developed southeast of Kyoto in Fushimi.

One of the most important documents in the history of saké is the *Tamon'in Nikki*, which gives a detailed account of saké brewing at the temple Kōfukuji in Nara. An entry dated 1599 outlines a schedule for spring brewing identical to the three-stage method employed today. Brewers had been using yeast for some time now, and this saké must have been extremely close to what is now called *seishu*, or "refined saké." More important, the *Tamon'in Nikki* reveals that saké brewers were already using the technique of *hi-ire*—pasteurization—nearly three hundred years before Pasteur's great discovery in France.

## The Edo Period and Townsman Culture

Ieyasu established the capital of his new shogunate in Edo (modern Tokyo), a village on a bay just north of the early medieval capital of Kamakura. In the 1630s the shogunate established a system under which feudal lords (daimyo) in the provinces were required to set up official residences in Edo and to live in the city every other year. It also closed the country to foreign contact and established a rigid class system based on Neo-Confucian concepts of government. The samurai or warrior class, who had been so involved in the shaping of the na-

Hideyoshi at his famous cherry-blossom-viewing banquet at Daigo, southeast of Kyoto, 1598.

中橋

Edo street scene. Most of the pavilions are restaurants or drinking establishments. (*Edo Meisho Zu-e*, 1830.)

tion, was at the apex of this structure followed by farmers, artisans, and merchants. The new era of peace, however, robbed the samurai of their military function, and as they assumed more and more the character of an urban bureaucracy they became a great class of consumers. And though the merchant class was at the bottom of the social hierarchy, it quickly came to play the leading role in the economy. In 1657, a great fire ravaged Edo. The rebuilding that followed led to the transformation of the city into a huge metropolis, with a population of over one million. In its time, Edo was the largest city in the world.

Saké brewers in Osaka and Kyoto were quick to capitalize on this new market. Some became rich and were celebrated in popular literature as paragons of diligence and ambition. One such man was Katsuya Saburō Uemon of the Kōnoike brewery in Ikeda, a suburb of Osaka, who made a fortune by sending saké to Edo on pack horses. This was a risky undertaking, because each horse could carry only two 53-liter casks, and the journey up the Tōkaidō highway to Edo required several weeks. But the bold plan paid off because Edo connoisseurs, mostly wealthy daimyo and officers of the new shogunate, were willing to pay almost any price for Kōnoike's luscious saké. It was wonderfully light—because it was made with highly polished rice—and already dominated the market in the

Osaka–Kyoto (Kansai) area. As the Edo trade developed and other producers began catering to the same taste, Kansai developed into Japan's major saké-brewing area, which it still is today.

Osaka was also the central collection point for tax rice. In 1624 Kōnoike Shinroku received a commission from the shogunate to establish ocean-shipping facilities on the island of Kujōjima at the mouth of the Yodo River in Osaka. Along with such famous entrepreneurs as Kinokuniya Mon'uemon, he began shipping saké to Edo in ships designed to carry rice. In 1723, saké merchants to the west in the nearby coastal area of Nada developed the famous *taru kaisen*, or "cask ships," specially designed for transporting saké. The rapid development of this system of ocean transportation favored Nada on the coast over its inland neighbors Ikeda and Itami. These older saké-producing areas continued to prosper, but Nada soon dominated the market in Edo. In 1785, Nada brewers shipped 24,000 kiloliters of saké to Edo. By 1823 that figure had risen to 42,000 kiloliters. By 1818, more than 300 cask ships were plying the sea lanes between Nada and Edo.*

---

*The Nada region included Imazu, Nishinomiya, Uozaki, Mikage, and Nishigō, coastal districts that are today part of the cities Kobe and Nishinomiya. The word Nada is still used to refer to the area and the large breweries headquartered there.

Saké wholesaler in Shinkawa, Edo. The structure in back is probably a warehouse. (*Edo Meisho Zu-e*, 1830.)

With the development of ocean transportation and the influx of saké from Kansai, a new type of merchant appeared in Edo, the wholesaler or *sake ton'ya*. These merchants built huge storehouses and docking facilities in Shinkawa and Kayabachō, and acted as wholesalers and agents for the large brewers in Nada, Fushimi, and Osaka. Following the example of their predecessors in the Muromachi period, the *sake ton'ya* collaborated with their clients in Kansai to establish a lucrative business in money lending and rice brokering. With their far-flung interests in shipping and commerce, saké merchants soon became the wealthiest in the land.

The Nada brewers were not just shrewd entrepreneurs. They were great, innovative saké makers. Most saké brewers at this time were producing saké from the autumn equinox to the spring equinox, and their sakés were distinguished by the period in which they were fermented. The most highly prized sakés were those produced in the very coldest months, when the mash could be kept at the optimum temperature for fermentation. In the early 17th century, brewers in Ikeda and Itami began to limit brewing to these times. These sakés were called *kan-zukuri no sake*, or "saké brewed in the cold months," and won great favor among Edo connoisseurs. The problem with *kan-zukuri* was that limiting the period of brewing meant limiting the amount of saké that could be produced in a single

Pot for heating saké. Edo period.

Rectangular wooden container used for storing saké before the invention of barrellike casks. Early Edo period.

Square wooden ladles used for measuring saké. A customer would take his own container to a shop to have it filled from a cask. Edo period.

Entryway of Matsui saké brewery. Kyoto.

year. During the period from 1789 to 1850, Nada
brewers gradually adopted the system of *kan-zukuri*,
but as they did they introduced new technologies
of mass production that ultimately enabled them
to reduce the period of brewing to the one hundred coldest days of the year without sacrificing their
outputs or incomes.

The scope of these innovations is truly astound-
ing. In the early 19th century Nada brewers replaced
foot-driven mills for polishing rice with mills
driven by waterwheels, reducing both the time and
labor required for this crucial job. They made the
wooden brewing and storage tanks bigger than ever
before and adapted the traditional implements of
saké brewing to large-scale production. Most important, they discovered that the water of the
Nishinomiya area, *miyamizu*, had special properties
that enabled brewers to use less of it with more
highly polished rice to produce at reasonable cost
a light, clear *kan-zukuri* saké that drove the Edo connoisseurs wild. The sakés of Nada became preeminent. All other sakés came to be disparaged as
"country sakés."

These major new developments in saké brewing
coincided with a great transformation of saké connoisseurship. In the early Edo period, only the
samurai frequented the pleasure quarters of the cities.
But as the city merchants became increasingly
wealthy, and as the government restricted more and
more the life styles of the samurai, the townsmen
emerged as the central figures in a new urban
culture. The Edo townsmen were frankly
hedonistic, and their art, literature, and concepts
of connoisseurship centered on the two "bad places"
of the Yoshiwara pleasure quarter and the Kabuki

Matsumoto saké brewery.
Fushimi, Kyoto.

Scene of an Edo-period drinking establishment. The man just inside the doorway is preparing fish. One samurai says to another "Let's have a drink!"

theater district, otherwise known as the "floating world." The samurai did not remain strangers to epicureanism for long, and soon began—often on funds borrowed from townsmen—to participate in these same pleasurable pursuits. Townsman cultures also flourished in the other great cities of Japan, the connoisseurs of Kyoto and Osaka taking great pride in the differences between their own sensibilities and the tastes of Edoites. Nevertheless, Edo was *the* city of connoisseurs, and just as the term *kudari-zake* ("saké sent down" to Edo) became synonymous with first-class saké, *Edomae* ("cuisine of Edo quality") was used on the signboards of restaurants throughout the country.

It is to the culture of the Edo-period townsmen that modern Japanese look for their standards of traditional Japanese taste. The townsmen defined *fūryū* within the complex world view of *iki*, a term that includes concepts of sophistication, urbanity, and taste and suggests a delicacy of sensibility that is difficult to imagine today.

The Edo-period connoisseur, or *tsūjin*, was expected to have an incredible range of knowledge—to recognize a song from a few notes plucked on a samisen; to know not only what foods (sakana) were

Courtesans on a boat on the river. The epitome of *fūryū*. (By Utamaro, Edo period.)

Of course, the inns and tea houses of the Edo-period pleasure quarters were accessible only to the wealthy few, and there were many other eating and drinking establishments catering to less affluent customers. At the bottom of the scale were the *izakaya* (literally, "sit-down saké shops"), where the poorest townsman could drink cheap saké at crude tables set up outside, with only a little salt, red pepper, or miso paste for sakana.

## Modernization

On July 8, 1853, Commodore Matthew Perry of the United States appeared in the harbor of Uraga south of Tokyo with four warships. This visit of the famous "black ships" put an end to a period of national isolation that had lasted for more than 250 years, and set the stage for a civil war that would result in the Meiji Restoration of 1868. The victors abolished the shogunate, established a new Western-style government under the Meiji emperor, and launched a program of westernization and modernization that quickly transformed Japanese society and culture.

With the opening of the country, Japanese of the Meiji period (1868–1912) adopted Western styles and tastes with an enthusiasm that bordered on hysteria. For a while it seemed that Japanese culture might disappear altogether. Gradually, however, a society developed in which things Japanese and

appropriate for a warm evening at the beginning of spring, but which particular delicacies would delight the eyes and the palate of his geisha companion. The ideal connoisseur was the man who would spend his entire fortune for a single night of pleasure. The geisha represented the feminine ideal in the world of *iki*. Her popularity and high status in the pleasure quarter was destined to be fleeting—thus, the floating world—but in her prime, the geisha matched the male *tsūjin* in refined sensibility and played a major role in setting standards of fashion, beauty, and elegance. It was no easy matter to meet these standards, and the literature of the period is full of stories that parody the rich country bumpkin or the benighted samurai attempting to make his way in the sophisticated world of the demimonde. Even today, there are very few Japanese who feel completely comfortable or know how to behave in the high-class inns, or *ryōtei*, of Tokyo's Akasaka district or Kyoto's Pontochō.

Signs of the times: eating beef and drinking saké. Beef was not generally eaten in Japan before the Meiji period. Note how the gentleman on the right has trimmed his samurai topknot and let his hair grow in the Western style. (Illustration from the novel *Agura-nabe*, by Kanagaki Robun, 1872–73.)

"Hairy ones"—foreigners, that is—enjoying a banquet with saké in Yokohama. (By Issen Yoshikazu, 1868.)

land owners quickly seized this opportunity, and by 1872 more than 30,000 new breweries had been established throughout the country. This was a difficult period for Nada and Fushimi. Annual shipments of saké from Nada to Tokyo (formerly Edo) dropped from a peak of over 1 million casks at the end of the Edo period to 500,000, as many Nada saké merchants reduced their brewing operations and turned increasingly to shipping and money lending for their profits.

The Meiji government was primarily interested in the saké industry as a source of tax revenues, and in the end its policies proved to be the salvation of the large, established makers. Large tax increases were declared every year until it became difficult for small brewers to remain in business. In 1881, after a particularly high tax hike in 1880, brewers in Kōchi Prefecture called for a national meeting of brewers to demand lower taxes. The more established makers wisely took a cool attitude toward this proposal and went along with the government's policies, concentrating on capital accumulation and modernizing their operations. As smaller breweries were forced out of business by the new tax system, the large makers steadily regained their lead. Nevertheless, while the number of brewers declined to around 8,000 by the turn of the century, many local brewers also accommodated themselves to the new system, and it was during this period that the present structure of the industry was established: large makers concentrated in Nada and Fushimi produce "national brands" that are available everywhere, while local brewers produce *jizake*, or local sakés, for regional markets.

The large makers handled the changing conditions by modernizing with a vengeance. They reorganized their breweries into modern corporate structures, introduced the most up-to-date technologies from the West, and reorganized their distribution systems and marketing strategies. When the market in Tokyo for Nada sakés shrank due to higher prices, for example, the large makers launched a successful campaign to break into other regional markets. With the implementation of the Trade Name Registration Law in 1884, these makers took advantage of their recognized brand names to begin advertising on a national basis. The famous cask ships were replaced first by modern sailing ships, then by steamers, and finally by rail transportation. By the turn of the century, the 1.8-

things Western each had their place. The true connoisseur of the Meiji period, and of all subsequent periods, was expected to be at home in both worlds—to enjoy the subdued ambience of a *ryōtei* as well as the elegant atmosphere of a French restaurant. The Meiji period established a pattern of cosmopolitan taste that Japanese would do well to remember today.

Like its predecessors, the Meiji government displayed a keen interest in the saké industry from the very beginning and instituted sweeping changes that threatened the domination of large makers. Under the tax and licensing system of the Tokugawa shogunate, the big breweries in Nada and Fushimi had enjoyed special privileges, and the entry of new brewers into the market had been strictly controlled. In 1871, the new government abolished this system and replaced it with one that allowed anyone who could afford it to pay licensing fees and taxes to enter the industry. Wealthy

Saké vats set out to dry at a Nada brewery in the
mid-1920s.

liter bottle (*isshō-bin*) began to replace bulky wooden
casks as the principal packaging container. Most important, the operations of the large makers quickly lost the aspect of traditional Edo-period breweries,
or *kura*, and took on the appearance of modern
Western factories. In all these developments, the
large makers were far ahead of their smaller com-
petitors, and this enabled them to secure a preeminent position during the boom years of the Taishō
period (1912–26). In 1919, despite new competition from beer, whiskey, and wine, total saké production reached its prewar peak of over 1 billion
liters, and Nada alone accounted for 10 percent of
this figure.

It was also during the Meiji period that a pattern of government regulation and active participa-
tion in the industry was established. In 1904, the
National Research Institute of Brewing, which now
has branches all over the country, was organized
as a testing and research institution under the
jurisdiction of the Treasury Ministry. It was soon
followed by research stations under the auspices of
prefectural governments. In 1907, the Treasury
Ministry cooperated with the Japan Saké Brewers
Association to sponsor the first National New Sakés
Competition. These competitions subsequently ex-
erted a profound influence on the industry in terms
of saké gradings and reputations.

A large saké cup to commemorate the war with
Russia in 1904–5, and a smaller one to mark
Japan's occupation of Manchuria in the early 1930s.
The pitcher, or *tokkuri*, dates from Japan's conflict
with China, just before the start of World War II.

Modern-day Japanese liquor store with saké, whiskey,
beer, juice.

## The War Years

The prosperity of the Tai-shō period came to an abrupt end in the second year of the Shōwa period (1926 to the present), when the Great Depression struck the entire world. During the next ten years, demand for saké plummeted, and many small local makers were forced into bankruptcy. The worst was yet to come. In 1937, war broke out in China, marking the beginning of a dark period of direct government controls, rationing, and shrinking production that would not end until after the American Occupation in 1952. In 1943, the government promulgated the "General Plan for Reorganization of the Refined Saké Industry," under which 3,340 of the 6,919 brewing facilities in operation at the time were converted into munition factories or forced out of business. Some 546 brewers were forced to suspend operations, and only 3,033 breweries remained open. Total saké production dropped 35 percent in a single year.

Wartime shortages resulted in new techniques of producing saké that would transform the industry. In the Japanese colony in Manchuria, rice was almost unavailable. Brewers there began to develop techniques of adding pure rectified alcohol, glucose, glutenous rice, and other ingredients to small quantities of rice mash so as to increase the yield of saké by three to four times; this was called "tripling the saké" (*sambai zōjōshu*). In 1941, they managed to create a completely synthetic saké that did not use rice at all. In 1942, brewers in Japan also began experimenting with adding alcohol to the final saké mash. The government recognized this practice in 1944, and it was soon being used throughout the country. Continuing shortages in the immediate postwar years led to its widespread adoption.

## Saké Today

The history of Japanese saké after World War II has been one of rapid modernization and increasing concentration of production in large automated factories. After a difficult period of reconstruction, the industry slowly began to recover around 1952. In 1955 total production once again reached prewar levels. In recent years, advances in thermodynamics, mechanical and electrical engineering, and computer technology have revolutionized the hardware of the industry, while research in microbiology, biochemistry, and genetic engineering have unlocked many of the secrets of the brewing process. The techniques of adding alcohol and other products,

Jaja Uma, a modern *yakitori* shop cum café bar. Fuchū, Tokyo.

Drinking in style at the "Super Restaurant" Time Machine, built around the theme "future for humanity." Takadanobaba, Tokyo.

originally employed as extreme measures during a period of shortages, are now in the mainstream of brewing technology.

The culture of saké has also been transformed. Drinking after hours at small downtown bars is a mainstay in the life of the Japanese male—and is being indulged in more and more by women, too. But often the drink of choice is not saké. In 1983, the share of saké in the total consumption of alcoholic beverages in Japan fell below 30 percent for the first time, while beer commanded a staggering 63 percent of the market. Saké is also being challenged by whiskey, wine, and another traditional Japanese beverage, *shōchū*, a distilled spirit resembling vodka.

In part, this is a result of affluence and the development of a determinedly cosmopolitan society with Western-style drinking venues. But many critics charge that the saké industry simply has not kept up with changing consumer tastes. In the 1960s and 1970s a rising consumer movement challenged the manufacturing and labeling practices of the industry and demanded a return to "real saké." Today, the popularity of natural foods has sparked a

resurgence of local sakés and an increased interest in brewing techniques and ingredients. Many of the attitudes represented by these trends are based on misconceptions, but the result has been increased competition, a concerted effort to respond to consumer demands, and a much more rational system of labeling.

After 1975, when the Japan Saké Brewers Association established a self-regulating system to enforce clearer labeling practices, the use of non-rice ingredients began to decline. This system was further strengthened in 1982, and there are clear signs that the industry has entered a period in which increasing pressure from consumers will force a shift of emphasis from quantity to quality. At the same time, the health-conscious younger generation is rediscovering saké, not only in its traditional context of Japanese-style restaurants and cuisine but as a great natural drink that can be enjoyed in any situation. If beer, whiskey, and wine are invading the elegant Akasaka *ryōtei* frequented by politicians and the corporate elite, saké is making a comeback in the jazz coffee shops and slick bars of Roppongi that are the nighttime haunts of the fashionable.

The first ingredient: pure water.

The second ingredient: rice.

The Kawai Shuzō brewery in Imai-chō, Kashihara City, Nara Prefecture. The building dates from the late 16th century.

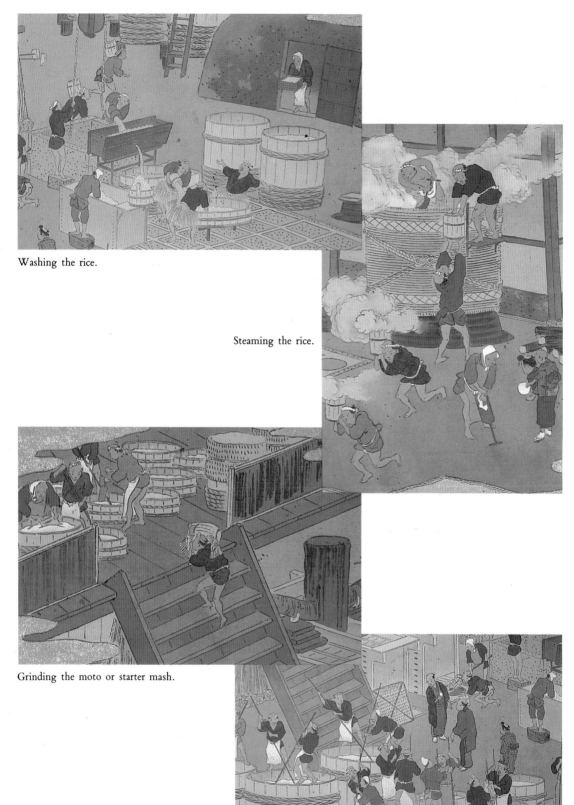

Washing the rice.

Steaming the rice.

Grinding the moto or starter mash.

Mixing the moromi or final mash.

# Saké
# Brewing

## Tōji: The Saké Brewmasters

Tōji are the master brewers of the traditional saké kura, the elite of a unique breed of artisans who trace their roots to the Edo period. As the practice of *kan-zukuri* grew more prevalent, the saké-brewing season became increasingly concentrated in the coldest months of the year. Kura owners in areas like Nada—some of whom took an active interest in brewing but who were mostly wealthy merchants or land owners— came to rely on outside groups of farmers or fishermen who were able to spend their unproductive months working away from home. These seasonal laborers were called the *kurabito*, ''people of the kura,'' or the *hyakunichi*, ''hundred dayers'' (a reference to the shortened period of brewing).

Among the *kurabito* was usually a leader from their home locality. Gradually there developed a complex and formal system in which these bosses, or tōji, played a central role, supervising all the details of the brewing and managing the work. The same tōji would work the same brewery each year. He in turn would pass his knowledge and rank on to his son, thus preserving the traditional art of saké making for generations.

The origin of the term tōji is hotly debated among saké historians. The most convincing theory is proposed by an Edo-period dictionary, *Wakun no Shiori*, which traces the term back to the Heian period, when women played the most important roles in the Shinto rituals that accompanied the saké brewing of the court. The *Engi Shiki* (905) refers to these women as tōji, and the *Wakun no Shiori* suggests that male saké brewers adopted this term during the Muromachi period. Even today, tōji observe the Shinto rituals of brewing saké, and it seems highly likely that the brewmasters of the Edo period preserved this time-honored title for their rank in the hierarchy of the *kurabito*.

By the early 19th century, tōji from particular regions had become associated with specific saké-producing areas. The most famous tōji were from Tamba and Tajima (modern Hyōgo Prefecture), and traditionally worked in the breweries of Nada. The breweries of Fushimi near Kyoto were supervised by tōji from Echizen (modern Fukui Prefecture) and Tango (near Osaka). While these old pre-Meiji place names formally disappeared with the modern geopolitical reorganization of Japan, tōji still use them in referring to themselves and the traditions their sakés embody.

Tamba tōji, for example, tell of the brewmaster Seibei, who in 1802 defied corrupt local officials and journeyed to Edo to win the right of oppressed Tamba peasants to work as *kurabito*. Seibei succeeded but was put under lifetime house arrest for

Tamba Tōji holding their annual purification ceremony at Matsuo Shrine, Kyoto, before the brewing season begins.

Steaming rice in a vat at a saké brewery in 1955.

defying the government's ban on travel. Today, all the members of the Tamba Tōji Association visit a monument to Seibei during their annual conclave in the fall, the high point of which is a Shinto purification ritual performed by a priest from Kyoto's Matsuo Shrine—another indication of how tōji traditionally credit their inspiration to the gods.

No matter how divine the inspiration, long years of practical experience, beginning with the most menial tasks, are required to learn the art of brewing. Traditional saké making requires the total involvement of all the *kurabito*, and long hours of manual labor. In the past, *kurabito* lived in the kura for the entire hundred days of the brewing season and were not allowed to go out at all once the mixing of the final mash had begun. Many of the steps in brewing took place at odd hours of the day and night. The youngest *kurabito* at the bottom were expected to get up at two o'clock in the morning to fix breakfast for the others. In modern Japan even the most conservative brewers have introduced machines to do the heaviest work, but saké brewing at the smaller kura still involves an irregular schedule, many menial chores, and a heavy dose of nearly feudalistic human relations. The *kurabito* in a traditional brewery who aspires to be a tōji must

experience all of this as he slowly makes his way up the hierarchy.

Today, many tōji work full time in small or medium-size breweries or in large companies, where they share the limelight with university-trained technicians. Of course, many modern tōji are technicians themselves, and an increasing number of them enter private industry as tōji after retiring from government research centers. Tōji continue to play an important role in organizing the industry's work force, and with the reemergence of small brewers, their role in setting standards of taste will become even more important.

## Water and Rice

Water and rice are the essential ingredients of saké. In some ways, they are the essential ingredients of Japan. Both were crucial to the survival of Japan's earliest agricultural settlements. Water in addition had purifying properties, and its liquid motions described the smooth and abundant flow of life in the universe. Rice, the staple food, was connected with fertility. The propitiatory festivals for seeding, planting, and the harvest defined the main contours of the Japanese year. In premodern times, a man's wealth was measured by the quantities of rice his

One of the sources of *miyamizu* on Mount Rokkō, above Nishinomiya.

lands produced. Some anthropologists say that Japanese life today is still served by the mentality of rice-paddy culture: a smooth-running social machine of shared symbols, public diligence, group effort, and sometimes bland conformity. No wonder that many Japanese people, when they drink saké, believe they are imbibing the very distillation of their earth and their spirit.

About 25 kiloliters of water are used for each ton of rice in saké making. The ideal water for brewing is colorless, tasteless, and odorless, and contains only trace amounts of minerals and organic substances. Just as wine connoisseurs speak of the waters of Bordeaux and beer drinkers of the waters of Munich, Pilsen, and Milwaukee, Japanese saké drinkers extol the virtues of *miyamizu*, the water of Nishinomiya, a port city in Nada. *Miyamizu* was discovered in 1840 by Yamamura Tazaemon, whose story is one of the important chapters in the history of traditional saké making.

Tazaemon owned kura in Nishinomiya and nearby Uozaki. Everyone agreed that the Nishinomiya kura produced better saké than the one in Uozaki, and Tazaemon wanted to know why. One year he replaced all the tools and equipment in Uozaki. The next year he brought in tōji from Nishinomiya. But

still the Uozaki saké did not improve. Finally, at enormous expense, he hired ox carts to transport enough water from his wells at Nishinomiya to brew one vat of saké at Uozaki. The other Nada brewers all laughed—until news came that Edo connoisseurs were willing to pay almost any price for the new brew. Soon everyone in Nada was using Nishinomiya water, buying it from the wells of farmers and other people traditionally outside the saké industry. Orders for the water even came from distant brewers. By 1895 more than 1 million casks of *miyamizu* were being shipped from Nishinomiya.

Modern chemical analysis and geology reveal what gives *miyamizu* its unique qualities. The well water of Nishinomiya comes from three sources: subterranean water from the nearby Shukugawa River, rich mineral water running down from Mount Rokkō, and sea water from Nishinomiya Bay. These waters mix below a thick layer of fossilized shells, and are filtered up through it as they rise to the surface. One example of how these waters conspire to make a good saké is the chemical reaction that occurs between the waters from the Shukugawa River and Mount Rokkō. The latter is rich in carbonates, phosphates, and potassium, all of which are important for the cultivation of yeast. But

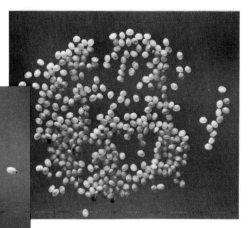

Unpolished brown "Gohyakumangoku" rice and the same rice polished 50 percent, used by the Utsunomiya Shuzō brewery for making its premium Shikizakura *ginjō* saké.

Mount Rokkō water also has a high concentration of iron, which can cause the saké to deteriorate. In *miyamizu* the iron is oxidized by acids in the water from the Shukugawa River, and then filtered out completely when the water passes through the fossil layer. Today, *miyamizu* is produced synthetically. Brewers also use aeration, filtration, and many other modern methods in order to improve the properties of their water.

The same Tazaemon is also credited with revolutionary innovations in the use of rice. The kind of rice used in saké (and in all Japanese cooking) is the short-grain Japonica variety that gets sticky and clingy when cooked. Rice for eating is polished about 15 percent, while rice selected for saké tends to be of larger grain and is polished more to remove proteins, lipids, and minerals from the surface that would destroy the clarity of the final brew. Before Tazaemon, the formula for the ratio of water to rice in the final mash had been 6 *tō* (108 liters) to 1 *koku* (150 kilograms). But after discovering *miyamizu*, Tazaemon hit upon the idea that the rice could absorb more water if he polished it more. He raised the amount of water to equal that of rice and ordered his brewmaster to polish the rice for three days and three nights before soaking it. Needless to say, the saké was a great success. It was also cost-effective, producing more saké out of less rice. Tazaemon's discovery was what enabled Nada to flourish as a big commercial brewing center, and it provided the germ of the idea for premium *ginjō* sakés, which would only be fully realized with the advent of super-efficient rice-polishing machines in the Meiji period.

Saké brewers today either grow their own rice or subcontract the work out to local farmers. Two-thirds of the rice used in saké in Japan is of the type called Yamadanishiki, originally from Hyōgo Prefecture. (California brewers use Rose rice grown in the United States.) Rice prices are artificially supported by the government to appease growers who

Mixing kōji spores with freshly steamed rice.

米をあらひの図

造酒丹伊

Washing the rice.

have been left behind as Japanese eating habits have changed to include more meat and dairy products. This in turn has eaten into saké makers' profits. Genetic engineering work, therefore, is proceeding apace in a constant search to improve yields without sacrificing clarity or flavor.

## The Traditional Art

Most saké produced in Japan today comes from huge modern factories such as those of the big makers in Nada and Fushimi, whose use of stainless steel vats, biochemistry, and computers have revolutionized the industry in many ways. The basic methods of brewing saké, however, have changed little from those used to make *morohaku* saké from polished rice at Tamon'in in the late 1500s, and small breweries here and there still cling to the old ways. They are a legacy of Japanese society in the Edo period, when diligent entrepreneurs pursued an independent course of modernization in isolation from the rest of the world for more than 250 years.

Modern science now provides explanations for the efficacy of techniques developed over centuries of observation and experimentation. The brewers of Tamon'in did not know that they had invented pasteurization in the process of *hi-ire*, but they did know that heating saké after it had been filtered would keep it from spoiling. This pattern of discovery was repeated over and over again until the perfection of "cold brewing," or *kan-zukuri*, in Nada in the 19th century, the most sophisticated traditional brewing process in the world. This section explains how it works.

### MULTIPLE PARALLEL FERMENTATION

What sets saké making apart from other brewing methods is the process that is now called multiple parallel fermentation, as opposed to simple fermentation in the case of wine and separate fermentation for beer. Fermentation occurs when sugar is converted to alcohol by yeast. The grape mash ("must") used in wine making contains a high percentage of sugar to begin with, so fermentation occurs spontaneously due to the yeast on the grape skins or involves only the addition of cultured yeast. In brewing fermented beverages from grain, it is necessary first to convert the starch in the grain to sugar, which will then be converted to alcohol by yeast. In the case of brewing beer, these two pro-

MULTIPLE PARALLEL FERMENTATION:
ALCOHOL AND GLUCOSE CONTENT IN THE
FINAL MASH. Action of the kōji enzyme changes the
starch in the rice to a sugar, which the yeast then
transforms into alcohol. Note that the glucose level never
exceeds 2 percent.

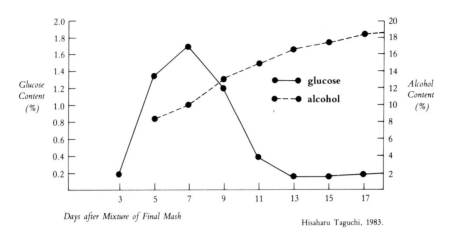

*Days after Mixture of Final Mash*

Hisaharu Taguchi, 1983.

cesses are separate. Saccharification and liquefaction are accomplished by adding malt to the grain mash; the resulting liquid is then fermented by adding yeast. Saké brewing combines these two processes, so that liquefaction of the mash and the conversions of starch to sugar and sugar to alcohol occur simultaneously. The result is that undiluted saké has an alcohol content of about 20 percent, higher than any other naturally fermented beverage. Fortified wines such as port or sherry have alcohol contents of 16–20 percent, but these are achieved by adding rectified alcohol to the must during fermentation.

The secret of saké brewing, then, is in the marriage of the kōji mold (*Aspergillum oryzae*), which produces enzymes that convert starch to glucose, and saké yeast (*Saccharomyces cerevisiae*), which is similar to the yeast used in brewing beer. To achieve an alcohol content of 20 percent, 40 percent of the starch in the rice must be converted to sugar. But a 40 percent concentration of sugar at the beginning of fermentation would suppress the metabolic function of the yeast and prevent it from multiplying, thus inhibiting the production of alcohol. Saké brewing gets around this by taking steamed rice, water, and steamed rice treated with the kōji mold and adding them in three separate stages to a highly concentrated yeast mash (*moto*). The temperature of the final mash (*moromi*) is kept down to around 15°C (59°F) as multiple parallel fermentation continues for a period of about eighteen days. The low temperature makes saccharification proceed slow-

ly, at an average rate of 2–4 percent a day. The yeast in the mash converts these small amounts of glucose into alcohol at the rate of 1–2 percent a day, so that the total glucose concentration never rises above 2 percent. The low concentration of glucose enables the yeast to multiply and spread rapidly until the concentration of alcohol reaches a level of about 20 percent.

POLISHING, STEEPING, AND STEAMING

Ordinary white rice for eating is polished until each grain is reduced 8–10 percent. Rice used in saké has larger grains and is reduced 25–30 percent, or, in the case of some premium sakés, more than 50 percent. Polishing removes proteins, lipids, and minerals that are more abundant toward the edge of the grain—these produce undesirable flavors in the final product and can also affect the way in which the kōji mold grows. More polishing thus results in a "cleaner" saké.

After the rice is polished and washed, it is steeped in a large vat of water until it has absorbed about 30 percent of the water. Steeping helps heat penetrate the grains in the next stage, and it accelerates the speed at which starch is changed to sugar. The rice is then transferred into a large wooden tub, called a *koshiki*, which has holes in the bottom to admit steam. The *koshiki* is placed over a metal tub of boiling water. In addition to sterilizing the rice, steaming ruptures the starch granules in the grain and makes them susceptible to kōji enzyme action. After fifty or sixty minutes,

其二 麹
醸

Steaming the rice (left) and making kōji.

the rice is removed from the *koshiki* and divided and cooled, depending on which of the stages of the brewing process it will be used in.

MAKING KŌJI RICE

The basic sequence in making saké is: (1) making kōji; (2) preparing the concentrated yeast mash, or moto; and (3) brewing, or *tsukuri*. Kōji—a mold—produces the diastatic enzyme, which converts starch to sugar, and the proteolytic enzyme, which breaks down proteins, as well as more than fifty other enzymes that are responsible for the aroma and taste of saké. Different colored varieties of kōji are also used in the manufacture of soy sauce and miso.

Because making the kōji rice is the first step in the brewing sequence and contributes so much to the ultimate success of the saké, it is one of the severest tests of the brewer's skill. First, he must choose the type of dried kōji spores to be used. All tōji have their favorite kōji brands, or, in some cases, may mix several brands that are known for particular qualities. The rice used in making kōji is also more refined than the bulk of the steamed rice that will be added later to the final mash.

After steaming, 20 percent of the rice is taken from the *koshiki* and cooled to about 30°C (86°F). Then the rice is taken to a special double-walled saunalike room that retains heat. Here, dried kōji spores are scattered over the surface of the rice and kneaded in to distribute them evenly. After a few hours the rice is moved to shallow wooden trays that are placed on shelves and covered with a cloth. The kōji mold begins to grow. As it grows, the temperature of the rice begins to rise. To ensure that the temperature of the rice does not get too high (it will eventually reach 40°C [104°F] or more) workers stir it twice every four hours. After forty to forty-five hours, the boxes containing kōji rice are removed from the warm kōji room so that the lower temperature outside will stop the growth of the kōji bacteria. After it has cooled, the kōji rice is light, dry, and flaky, and has an odor suggestive of roast chestnuts.

Kōji rice that will be used in making moto, or "starter," is produced in the same way, but the process is prolonged somewhat so that the concentration of enzymes is even higher.

MOTO: THE SEED MASH

While it comprises less than 10 percent of the rice

TORORI TORORI-TO!
THE MOTO WE GRIND
WE MAKE INTO SAKÉ
AND THEN WE SHIP IT TO EDO!
WELL, EVEN IN EDO
IT'S THE PREMIUM BREW,
IF IT'S SAKÉ YOU ASK FOR,
SAY ''KEMBISHI OTOKOYAMA''!

NOW SEE HOW THE MAIDEN PUTS UP HER HAIR
AND RESTS BENEATH BLOSSOMING CHERRIES:
TELL ME, WHICH IS THE MAIDEN,
AND WHICH ARE THE FLOWERS?

—from the ''Grinding the Moto'' song

used in a single batch of saké, the seed mash called moto is the starter of the brewing process, for it is the yeast crop grown in the moto that converts the sugar produced by the enzymes in kōji into alcohol.

The oldest method of producing this yeast mash is called *mizu moto* (''water moto'') or *Bodai moto*, after the great temple complex on Mount Bodai near Nara where it was discovered in the late middle ages. About 3 kilograms of steamed rice that has already been infected by yeast from the air is sealed in a cloth bag and buried in a large cask of uncooked polished rice (87 kilograms), to which is added about 130 liters of water. After four or five days, the water becomes cloudy, begins to bubble, and develops an acid taste. The water, which contains saké yeast, is filtered off, and the polished rice is then steamed. A second mash is then made with the yeasty water, all of the steamed rice, and an additional 40 kilograms of kōji rice; in about five days the moto is ready for use. Moto produced by this method unfortunately contains a high concentration of lactic acid bacteria, which makes for a very sour saké. This technique fell into disuse around the 1920s.

After the Nada makers perfected their *kan-zukuri* saké in the late Edo period, a method called *kimoto*, or ''raw moto'' became dominant. Like the older method, this method relies on the properties of kōji and natural yeast in the air to produce the yeast mash.

The traditional mixture for this mash is 75 kilograms of steamed rice, 30 kilograms of kōji rice, and 108 liters of water. This mixture is divided among sixteen shallow wooden tubs about 70 centimeters in diameter. It is made in early evening and allowed to set throughout the night, with tōji stirring the mixture every three or four hours until morning to ensure that the water and rice are mixed thoroughly. From early morning on the next day until well into the afternoon, tōji ''grind'' the moto (*moto suri* or *yamaoroshi*). Using long bamboo poles with attached wooden paddles they rub the steamed rice and kōji rice against the bottom of the wooden tubs until the grains of rice are reduced to about one-third their original size and the mash assumes the consistency of a thick paste. This accelerates the activity of the kōji in converting the starch in the mash to sugar. Part of the lore of the tōji is music, and the ''grinding the moto'' song is sung in unison by the sixteen men who do this work. By the time the song has ended, many hours after it began, the mash should be at just the right consistency.

This paste is then allowed to set overnight and be chilled by the night air. In the morning the contents of the wooden tubs are poured into a large wooden vat. The mash is left here for two or three days, ideally at a temperature of about 8°C (46°F). For several more days after this, workers drop sealed buckets of hot water (*dakidaru*) into the mash, gradually raising its temperature and starting the cultivation of airborne yeast as the kōji converts the starch in the mash to glucose. When the temperature of the mash reaches 15°C (59°F), the mash takes on a sweet and acid taste, indicating that the yeast is propagating on its own. The yeast produces alcohol and carbon dioxide from the sugar, the mash begins to bubble and swell, and a temperature of around 25°C (77°F) is maintained without inserting *dakidaru*. After twenty to twenty-five days of fermentation, the moto mash has an extremely high concentration of pure saké yeast and is ready to be used as the starter for the main mash.

Modern biochemistry reveals the extent to which this traditional method of producing the yeast mash achieves a high degree of perfection. In the early stages, it encourages the rapid growth of lactic acid bacteria. These bacteria produce lactic acid, which inhibits the growth of unwanted bacteria. Later on in the process, the lactic acid and the alcohol produced by the yeast kill off the lactic acid bacteria, as well as unwanted wild yeasts, resulting in an extremely pure starter mash.

In the early 20th century, brewers discovered two new methods of making moto. The method of *yamahai moto*, or *yamaoroshi haishi moto* ("moto without *yamaoroshi*"), is based on the same principles as raw moto but eliminates the step of grinding the moto by first mixing pure kōji rice with water to accelerate the process of saccharification and then adding steamed rice. This method was originally used in relatively warm areas, but soon became the most common technique of producing moto naturally.

The second new method, called *sokujō moto*, or "fast-fermenting moto," was developed at the National Research Institute of Brewing in 1909 and is also based on the same principles as raw moto. The quantities of steamed rice, kōji rice, and water are about the same as in the raw moto process. The kōji rice is mixed with the water, and lactic acid is added to

a level of 0.5 percent, again to prevent the growth of unwanted bacteria that could adversely affect the flavor of the saké. At the same time, pure cultured saké yeast is added as "seed yeast." The steamed rice is then mixed in, and the mixture is allowed to cool for two or three days. Then *dakidaru* are used to raise the temperature gradually to 20°C (68°F), the optimum temperature for the growth of yeast. Sometime between the fifth and eighth days, the mash begins to swell and bubble. This mash is ready to use as a starter for the main mash after ten to fifteen days, compared with nearly a month for raw moto.

MOROMI: THE FINAL MASH

When the kōji rice and the moto are ready, the moromi, or final mash, is mixed over a period of four days. The process of mixing the moromi is unique to Japanese saké brewing, and is called *sandan shikomi*, or "mixing in three stages." Traditionally, the moromi is mixed in large, open wooden vats with a capacity of 7 to 20 kiloliters. Increasingly large amounts of rice, kōji rice, and water are added to the moto on the first, third, and fourth days. No additions are made on the second day. The proportion of the additions relative to the moto is increased from 1 to 1 on the first day, to 2 to 1 on the third day, and to 4 to 1 on the fourth day, with each maker adapting the formula slightly to suit its own needs.

This seemingly simple process conceals important secrets. It must have required years of trial and error for traditional brewers to learn the importance of the second day, when the mash is allowed to set with no additions. This halt in the process is called *odori*, a term which refers to taking a mo-

| | Moto | 1st Addition | 2nd Addition | 3rd Addition | (4th Addition) | Total |
|---|---|---|---|---|---|---|
| Total Rice (kg) | 210 | 470 | 850 | 1,470 | | 3,000 |
| Steamed Rice (kg) | 140 | 330 | 650 | 1,230 | | 2,350 |
| Kōji Rice (kg) | 70 | 140 | 200 | 240 | | 650 |
| 30% Brewer's Alcohol (l) | | | | | 1,200 | 1,200 |
| Water (l) | 230 | 420 | 1,010 | 2,030 | 360 | 4,050 |

QUANTITIES OF INGREDIENTS AT EACH STAGE OF MIXING THE MOROMI. Traditional brewers mix the final mash in three stages. The fourth addition of alcohol and water is a controversial postwar development.

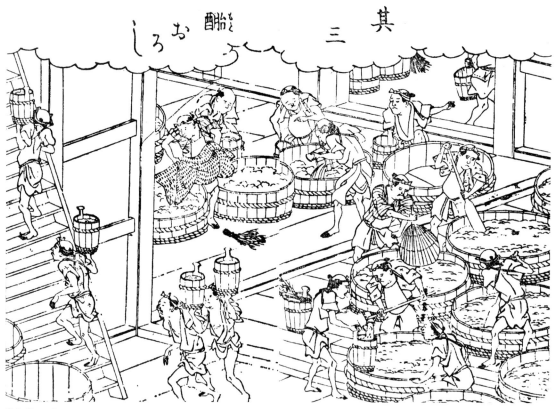

しろ醪を摺 三 其

Grinding the moto.

ment's rest at the foot of a staircase to gather strength for the ascent. Brewers learned that the concentration of yeast in the mash becomes almost as high during the second day as that of the moto itself.

The addition of rice, kōji rice, and water on the third day is called *nakazoe* ("middle addition"). Things are in a delicate balance at this stage. On the first and second days, the temperature of the mash is allowed to rise to 14°–15°C (57°–59°F) in order to encourage the growth of the yeast. The mixing vat is left uncovered, but the acids being produced in the mash suppress the growth of unwanted bacteria. Then, when the large addition on the third day reduces the acidity of the mash, the temperature is lowered to 9° or 10°C (50°F) to suppress bacterial growth but still permit the yeast to multiply gradually. The final addition on the fourth day is called *tomezoe* ("stopping addition").

The next fifteen to eighteen days until fermentation is completed are a struggle with temperature. The growth of yeast and the various changes over the course of fermentation raise the temperature of the mash, and the brewer must judge when to force the temperature down. If the temperature gets too

high, fermentation and liquefaction can get out of hand, and proceed too rapidly. If the temperature is forced too low, they may proceed too slowly. In either case, the balance of multiple parallel fermentation is destroyed.

Before the advent of thermometers and temperature control, brewers relied on a wide range of techniques to determine and regulate the temperature of the mash. One of these was based on the characteristic bubbles that form on the mash during the various stages of fermentation as the yeast multiplies, attaches itself to the solids in the mash, and produces carbon dioxide. Already on the day after the final addition, fine, stringy bubbles appear on the top of the mash, and by the third day the mash looks as if it were covered with soap suds. The bubbles increase in size and density until fermentation begins to slow, and finally begin to recede. The changing appearance of these bubbles is one of the most important clues for the brewer in determining the progress of fermentation. Brewers also judged the mash by its taste and flavor at various stages.

The need to control temperature, and especially to be able to lower it when fermentation seemed

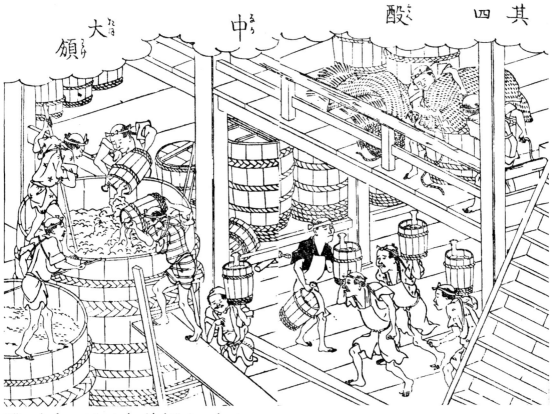

大
なみ
頒ね
中
える
其
四
酸い

Filling the fermentation tank with kōji rice and water.

to be getting out of hand, was the most important factor in the development of *kan-zukuri* in the Edo period. Old-style brewers today still work in the winter months, although modern techniques, including refrigeration, now allow saké production to continue throughout the year at the large makers. Traditional temperature control takes a wide variety of forms. One old-style kura still operating in Hyōgo Prefecture has windows in the brewing room whose lower sashes are at the level of the top of the brewing tank. The brewer says he regulates the temperature of the mash by opening and closing the window, sometimes as often as every five or ten minutes. Needless to say, the success of brewers in employing these traditional techniques depends on their skill, experience, and instinct, and often it is the last of these that makes a brewer famous.

### FILTERING

After the final mash has fermented for fifteen to eighteen days, the high concentration of alcohol in the mash causes the yeast to weaken, and fermentation begins to taper off. The moromi must now be filtered, and the decision as to when to do so is another test of the brewer's skill. If the yeast is left in the mash too long it will die, and its constituent elements will liquefy and enter the saké, producing an off-odor when the saké is aged. When the brewer feels that fermentation has gone far enough, the mash is loaded into long narrow sacks made of heavy brownish cotton waterproofed with persimmon tannin. Dozens of these sacks are stacked up side by side in a large, rectangular wooden container called a *sakafune* (''saké boat''). When weight is applied on top of the stacks, the saké filters down through the cotton and drips out from a spigot at the bottom of the *sakafune* into a well at its base. The fresh saké in the well is called *shinshu*, or ''new saké.'' The lees that remain in the filtering sacks are called *sake kasu*, and are marketed for use in pickling vegetables and in cooking.

### PASTEURIZATION AND AGING

Before anything is done to it, new saké is allowed to sit for about ten days at a low temperature, during which time continued enzyme reactions increase the amount of glucose and acids. It is then pasteurized (*hi-ire*) at a temperature of 60°C (140°F). Immediately afterwards the saké is transferred to

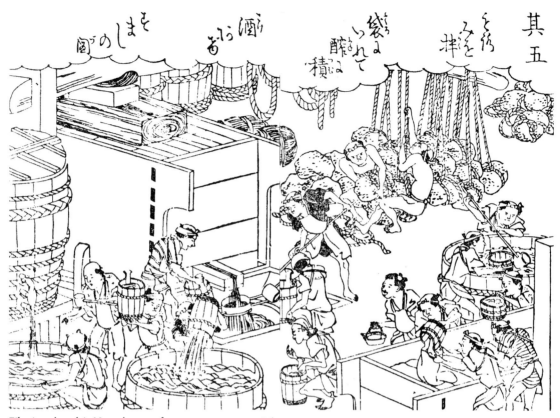

Filtering the saké. Note the use of stones as a counterweight.

sealed aging vats, traditionally made of Japanese cedar, where it is aged for six months to one year. New saké has a lemon color, smells strongly of kōji, and has a rather harsh taste. As the saké ages, its color gradually changes to a light amber, and its nose and taste take on a characteristic mellowness. It will also take on some of the flavor and fragrance of the wooden cask.

BLENDING

The final step in traditional brewing is often called "marrying the sakés," and it is a most subtle and mysterious art. The sakés from each batch of moromi are aged separately. Each vat has its own unique character, with strengths and weaknesses in a whole range of different categories of appraisal. It is the brewer's last chore to blend the various batches to create a final product that matches exactly his ideal flavor and aroma. In modern times chemical analysis does the job. But in olden days the master brewer had only his intimate knowledge of each of the sakés he had made and his own vision of the "saké of dreams" to guide him. Before bottling, the brewer will add water to dilute the saké to a level of between 15 and 17 percent alcohol.

## Modern Saké Brewing

With gleaming ultra-modern factories at one extreme and tiny local kura adhering to traditional techniques in darkened sheds at the other, saké brewing today is characterized by a great diversity of techniques. Even the most conservative brewers have been forced to replace traditional wooden tools and manual labor with stainless steel and electric power, and most brewers are actively introducing automation and new technologies into their operations. But even the high-tech factories of Nada and Fushimi, with their automatic kōji- and moto-making machines, continue to employ the basic three-stage process of sandan shikomi.

The small, local brewers who continue to produce saké in the coldest months of the year rely on tōji, the traditional brewmasters, to supervise a seasonal work force. Factory operations that produce saké all year round employ workers on a fulltime basis and entrust the supervision of increasingly complex production systems to highly trained technicians. For smaller brewers, the switch from the first of these patterns to the second often occurs with the retirement or death of a famous tōji whose skill and inspiration had made it possible for the owner to preserve traditional techniques.

It is only fair to point out that the most controversial modern brewing practices have nothing to do with the size of a brewery, or whether it uses "authentic" wooden vats or stainless steel and computers. These are the techniques of adding rectified alcohol (brewer's alcohol) to the final mash before filtering and of "tripling the saké"(*sambai zōjō-shu*), which were both developed during World War II. Almost all brewers add alcohol to sakés destined for the mass market. Purists condemn this practice, but brewers argue that the added alcohol combines with other ingredients in the final mash to produce the lighter, more drinkable sakés that consumers prefer after filtration and aging. They also point out that the same practice is employed in producing Scotch whiskeys and fortified wines.

"Tripling the saké" is even more controversial. Developed during the war by brewers in Manchuria to cope with shortages of rice there, the basic technique can conceivably produce completely synthetic saké with no rice at all. The modern brewers who employ it don't go that far, however, and instead prepare a flavoring solution of rectified alcohol, brewer's sugar (glucose), lactic acid, and monosodium glutamate that is added to the final mash as a "fourth addition" at some point in the last few days of fermentation. The effect is to boost the yield of the batch. Connoisseurs and the consumer movement insist that the ingredients of saké should be rice, kōji rice, and water, and if they are opposed to the practice of adding alcohol, they are inspired to wrath by the technique of "tripling the saké."

In fact, this is similar to the controversy over chaptalization (the addition of sugar) in brewing wine, which is permitted in all countries except Italy. It is a misconception that additions of sugar to the final mash make sakés sweet—the sugar is converted to alcohol. Nevertheless, strong pressure from the consumer movement has resulted in a marked decline of this practice, especially after 1975, when the Japan Saké Brewers Association instituted self-regulatory rules requiring brewers to list these ingredients as "brewer's sugar" 醸造用糖類. For example, Gekkeikan and Kiku-Masamune, two of the largest makers, announced in 1981 that they were voluntarily discontinuing the practice.

Another controversial technique involves a much

The Kawajiri brewery in Takayama, Gifu Prefecture. The building dates from 1840 and is still in use.

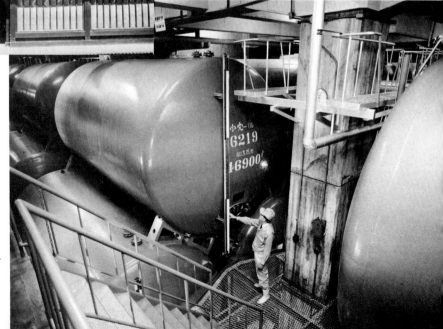

Modern saké storage tank in Nada.

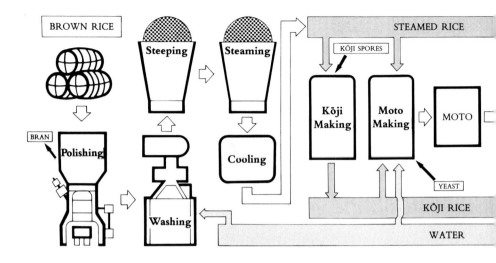

BROWN RICE · Steeping · Steaming · STEAMED RICE · KŌJI SPORES · Kŏji Making · Moto Making · MOTO · BRAN · Polishing · Cooling · YEAST · Washing · KŌJI RICE · WATER

more subtle distinction. As we have said, the rice used in saké is more highly polished than ordinary white rice. However, the white powder that collects beneath the sifting screen of a polishing machine is still 100 percent rice, and many modern brewers use this waste rice to produce a concentrated glucose solution that is added to the final mash. Of course, consumers pointed out that there is little point in talking about how highly polished the rice used in saké is if the white waste rice is going to be saccharified and added to it later. "White waste rice glucose solution" did not have to be listed as a non-rice ingredient until 1982, when the Japan Saké Brewers Association revised its self-regulatory rules to require makers to designate it as brewer's sugar on labels.

Increasing concentration of the industry, especially after a big push for modernization among the large makers in 1962, gave rise to the hotly debated practice called *okegai*, a system of subcontracting in which large makers buy bulk quantities of saké from smaller brewers throughout the country to blend with their own sakés. The large makers themselves were not prepared for the domination of the market they achieved after 1962, and found that they were unable to supply the rapidly increasing demand for their brands. At the same time, many smaller brewers could not compete in the new market structure and relied increasingly on subcontracting to stay in business.

Saké-producing regions in Japan are not as distinctly identified as wine-producing regions in Europe, but major scandals erupted in the early 1970s when the mass media reported that less than half of some sakés bearing the brand names of famous Nada and Fushimi makers was brewed by the companies themselves. The makers argued that their contracts with subcontractors contained strict specifications of ingredients and brewing methods, and that subcontractors were under the close supervision of their own quality-control experts. The practice of *okegai* continues, as does the debate, but the situation has improved considerably as large makers have expanded their own brewing facilities and small brewers have reasserted themselves in the expanding market for local sakés.

The most striking feature of the modern saké industry in general is the widespread application of advances in science and technology. Since the Meiji period, industry associations have maintained a close, symbiotic relationship with government research centers, such as the National Research Institute of Brewing in Ōji, northern Tokyo. New developments are quickly exploited to improve brewing techniques. A good example of this relationship is the development of the Association yeast system. Under this system, the Japan Saké Brewers' Association cooperates with national and prefectural research centers to collect samples of outstanding natural yeasts discovered in kura and factories throughout the country. The Association administers the storage and production of pure

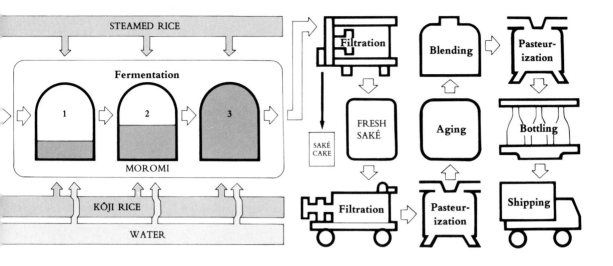

cultivated yeasts obtained from these, and distributes their seed cultures to saké makers.

Since the late 1950s, the great majority of saké makers, both large and small, have taken advantage of this system to eliminate their dependence on airborne yeasts and switch to the "fast-fermenting" method of making the seed mash. There is a wide variety of Association yeasts. The most widely used Association yeasts are Association No. 6 and No. 7, which were isolated from the final mashes of factory-produced sakés by technicians of the National Research Institute of Brewing in 1935 and 1946, respectively. Association No. 9 and No. 10 were isolated from the final mashes of elite *ginjō* sakés, making it possible for any brewer to produce their applelike bouquet, once the rarest and most sought for accomplishment in saké making.

The Association also cooperates with technicians in the National Research Institute of Brewing, prefectural research centers, and the industry in conducting research on new yeasts. For example, Association No. 10 and No. 7 were successfully crossbred to produce a new yeast that has the characteristic *ginjō* bouquet of the former and the strong fermentation qualities of the latter. This new yeast gave birth to the first full-bodied *ginjō* sakés. Other experimental yeasts have been produced by crossbreeding saké yeasts and wine yeasts, and there is already a "wine-type" saké on the market. The application of genetic engineering concepts to the production of new saké yeasts is only a step away.

The availability of pure cultivated yeasts and advances in thermodynamics have led to a new moto-making process that is twice as fast as the "fast fermenting" method. In this process, called *kōon tōka moto*, or "high-temperature saccharification moto," the moto mash is mixed and raised to a temperature of 55°C (131°F), the ideal temperature for rapid liquefaction and changing starch to sugar. After saccharification has proceeded for five to eight hours, lactic acid is added and the mash is cooled to about 20°C (68°F), at which point pure cultivated yeast is added. The entire process takes only five to seven days.

In some automated factories, this technique is being applied to the entire brewing process, eliminating the system of mixing in three stages altogether. Essentially, this approach is very similar to the process of brewing beer described above: saccharification and liquefaction precede fermentation, which is in turn regulated by automatic temperature control, instant chemical analysis, and data processing.

Similar innovations have revolutionized every other aspect of brewing saké. Computer-controlled kōji-making machines have taken the place of the kōji room even in some of the most traditional breweries, and new filtering devices and activated charcoal are replacing the old wooden saké boats. Even the famous waters of traditional saké-brewing regions, such as Nada's *miyamizu*, can now be pro-

Machine used in a modern brewery for steaming rice.

Saké fermentation tanks.

Bottling line in a saké brewery.

duced synthetically. Science and technology have done away with some of the mystery and romance of saké brewing, but they have also made it possible to produce better sakés than ever before. As we have seen, any brewer can now obtain the *ginjō* yeasts, with the happy result that these premium sakés are becoming available on the general market, sometimes even at affordable prices.

While small kura using traditional techniques compete today with technicians using computers and data processing in large automated factories, the challenges facing the saké industry affect all brewers, regardless of size. In the past, partly due to the influence of wartime and postwar shortages, scientific and technological advances were often exploited to increase production, with little concern for the traditional flavors of saké. The reemergence of local sakés is evidence of the fact that consumers are becoming more sophisticated; increasingly, they are demanding a return to the traditional taste.

The extent to which a saké achieves the traditional taste, however, does not depend as much on the scale of the brewery or the equipment used as on the ingredients and brewing techniques. Large makers do produce fine pure rice sakés, and some of them have led the industry in giving up objectionable practices. By the same token, small brewers can add alcohol and other non-rice ingredients to the final mash of their sakés as easily as large makers. It is true today that the full range of sakés is to be found in local sakés, and that the sakés of the large makers tend to differ only within a fairly narrow range of tastes. But the situation is changing rapidly. Small local brewers have opened up a market for high-quality, relatively expensive sakés, such as *ginjō*, and the large makers are beginning to exploit their technological advantage to produce excellent sakés on a profitable mass-market basis.

# Saké and the Japanese

A late-night prowl through the streets of any major city in Japan reveals a face of the Japanese very different from the one of diligent sobriety usually portrayed by Western analysts of the economic miracle. Blue-suited office workers stand arm in arm on sidewalks, singing of cherry blossoms and lost love. A lone construction worker staggers a meandering trail through city traffic. There in a recessed entryway, back to the crowd, is an electronics firm section chief engaged in a common form of civil pollution while chattering on about the foibles of his coworkers. In the trains, howeward bound at last, packed hordes of the feverishly unsteady intone as if in single chorus, "This time for sure, I am giving up saké!"

A subject of much happy conversation in bars recently was the announcement by a Japanese researcher that the Japanese are physiologically indisposed to alcoholism. The average Japanese body, it is claimed, lacks the particular enzyme that is the bane of heavy drinkers elsewhere. I'll drink to that, you say? The flip side of this situation seems to be that the Japanese body is inordinately susceptible to inebriation. Often, a single glass of saké is all that is needed to transform a taciturn face into a bright red bubble of warmth. Oh. You'll drink to that, too?

While it is true that today most Japanese drinkers would be as likely to choose beer or whiskey as saké, it is still the saké tradition that sets the style of imbibing in Japan. Beer, for example, is served to a table in large bottles, and the members of a party pour for each other in turn—which over the centuries is exactly how saké has been drunk at formal banquets. Whiskey, available mostly in Western-style lounges and bars, is similarly brought to the table in a full bottle, along with an ice bucket, mineral water, and swizzle stick. Someone in the party, or a hostess, then proceeds to mix all the drinks and pass them out. Market researcher George Fields, in his recent book *From Bonsai to Levis*, remarks on this custom and suggests that one reason certain drinks don't catch on in Japan is that they don't lend themselves to the tradition of sharing. A whiskey and water, which is ceremoniously mixed at the table, is far more popular in Japan than, say, a cocktail, which is concocted behind a bar and merely dispensed.

The word "saké" (or honorifically, "o-saké") is itself a generic term referring to any alcoholic beverage. The fermented-rice saké under discussion in this book is more precisely called *Nihon-shu*, the "wine of Japan," and it is this latter beverage that is clearly in evidence at the events and ceremonies that punctuate the typical Japanese year. There are cherry-blossom-viewing parties, moon-viewing parties, snow-viewing parties, and the ideal here is to get fueled up on saké and drunk on nature, spontaneously erupting into poem (in days gone by) or song (now accompanied by pre-recorded music).

Sumo wrestler Takanohana with a big saké cup being filled to celebrate his victory in the 1975 Osaka tournament.

The ideals of saké connoisseurship are inextricably linked to Japanese ideals of beauty and refinement.

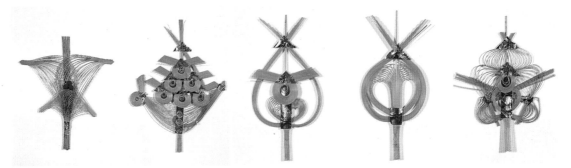

Bamboo *mikikuchi* for inserting in sacramental saké vessels offered to the household gods at New Year's.

At a traditional Shinto-style marriage, bride and groom consecrate their vows by the ritual of *san-san kudo*, drinking from the same saké cup three times.

Lacquer set for serving medicinal saké, or *o-toso*, at New Year's. A packet of various spices and medicines is steeped in premium saké on New Year's Eve. The saké is drunk the next morning for good health and long life.

In traditional wedding ceremonies, the ritual exchange of saké between the bride and the groom solemnizes their marriage. At the reception afterward, the newlyweds break open a cask of saké before all the assembled guests. At the celebration after a big national sumo tournament, the victorious jumbo wrestler is presented with a gigantic metal saké cup for him to drain with a single mighty effort. At building-site dedications, ceremonies marking the establishment of a new enterprise, festivals, New Year's celebrations, graduations, and fishing trips, there is inevitably a bottle of saké on hand to be shared and to bestow on the occasion a benediction. For saké in the earliest days was, like poetry, music, and everything else of the native tradition, considered a gift of the Shinto gods and was produced and enjoyed in their presence.

Still today, for example, in the farming villages of western Japan's Noto peninsula, each household has its own guardian god that protects its fields and rice paddies from early spring until harvest in the fall. After harvest, these gods return to their respective households to rest in small altars that have been prepared for them. It is at this time each year that the head of each household performs Ae no Koto, the ritual of feasting the god.

After dressing himself in traditional vestments that have been passed down in his family for generations, the household head goes to the door to greet the homecoming god. The god enters, and the household head says to him, "Please help yourself to a hot bath." When the god emerges from the bath, the household head awaits him with a formal stand laden with saké and small plates of food. "This," he says, "is the dry saké you are so fond of, and the food is your favorite spiced sweet potato. Thanks to you, the crop was splendid this year." Finally he offers the god a bowl of rice from the new harvest. When the god has eaten his fill, the household head bids him to retire to his resting place on the family altar, where he will remain until work in the fields begins again in the spring.

Such a ritual performed today, and the other ceremonies we have mentioned, represent an aspect of saké culture that is little removed from its most ancient form. But one can trace other branches of saké culture and discover that saké is at the soul of both Japanese cuisine and many forms of ceramic art. One finds it in theater and literature, at the root of murder and passion and ruin. Saké played

Spectators at a Kabuki performance. Customers sit in separate booths and partake of a set lunch, served with saké. (*Kabuki-zu Byōbu*, Edo period.)

Scene of early Edo-period commoners enjoying saké along a riverbank, possibly in Edo or Osaka. Eating fresh fish and imbibing in the grand style started about this time. (*Kawaguchi Yūri-zu Byōbu*, Edo period.)

Scene from the Kabuki play *Narukami*: A lady-in-waiting offers saké to a priest. She hopes to bring him to ruin and thus break his evil spell that holds the rain-giving dragon captive.

Apprentice geisha dancing at a traditional-style banquet in Kyoto's Gion district.

Popular actress Ai Kanzaki and voice coach Kyōkei Ōmoto, enjoying their saké.

an important part in Japan's economic foundation during medieval times, and it was the fuel that burned so brightly during the heyday of Japan's richly hedonistic popular culture in the Edo period. Connoisseurship, we recall, extended well beyond the mere act of drinking and demanded a sophisticated set of taste perceptions and manners, an openness to the fullness and potential of every moment. The quiet man of taste, subtle distinction, and sensitivity to the shifting world around him is still embodied in the saké connoisseur today.

True connoisseurship is, alas, on the decline in Japan. Or perhaps it is truer to say that, in Japan's affluent society, the superficial trappings of connoisseurship are easily available to anyone with a pocketful of money. The modern ''floating world'' of the big-city entertainment districts is more raunchy raree-show than robust and refined. The one-dimensional escapism of game parlors, Turkish baths, and tawdry, over-priced cocktail lounges pales in comparison with the more resonant thrill the true man of taste receives when he hits upon the perfect brew and the perfect food.

The role of saké and drinking in Japan nevertheless remains of practical importance. In a hierarchic, conformist society, rewards are promised to one who over the long term harmonizes his personal ambitions with the needs of his group. Drinking saké together after work—either with colleagues or clients—manages, through the ritual of sharing and cutting loose, to keep all the social cement in place even while it offers a forum for exorcising individual demons free of the leadenness of polite speech and decorum that so permeates every other Japanese social situation.

In principle, wives and the general public are understanding. Drink is duty. A man who creates a ruckus on a late-night binge may, when apprehended and cooled off, be asked to write a formal letter of apology. He will begin, ''I was drinking saké. . . .''

Few people in Japan would need to hear more.

THE MILLET WE OFFER
IS VERY CLEAN,
THE SAKÉ WE GIVE IS PURE.
O GREAT GODS!
LOOK DOWN AND BEHOLD THIS,
AND GRANT US YOUR MYRIAD BLESSINGS.
　　　　—from an ancient Shinto prayer

Stone god in Chichibu, western Tokyo, seated atop a saké cask and wearing a saké cup on its head.

# PART 2
# Principles of Connoisseurship

Various stoneware saké vessels.

Saké container made from a dried gourd. In olden days such containers sometimes served as hip flasks.

Ceremonial bucket, or *tsunodaru*, used since the Edo period for presenting saké at marriages and other celebrations.

Lacquer *katakuchi*, for pouring saké.

Arita ware, Saga Prefecture.

Mashiko ware, Tochigi Prefecture.

Hagi ware, Yamaguchi Prefecture.

Shigaraki ware, Shiga Prefecture.

Kiyomizu ware, Kyoto.

Tamba ware, Kyoto.

Kutani ware, Ishikawa Prefecture.

Tobe ware, Ehime Prefecture.

1. *Red sun*. Mix 1 ounce saké to 2 ounces tomato juice. Stir. Serve over ice with garnish of parsley.

2. *Saké screwdriver*. Place two or three ice cubes in a glass. Cover with saké. Fill to top with orange juice. Stir well and serve.

3. *Saké manhattan*. Mix 1 part dry saké with 2 parts rye whiskey. Add ice. Stir. Strain and serve with cherry in cocktail glass.

4. *Saké martini*. Mix 1 part dry saké with 1 part dry gin. Pour over cracked ice. Shake. Strain and serve with olive.

5. *Saké sour*. Place two or three ice cubes in a glass. Cover with saké. Fill to top with soda water. Serve with cherry and sliced lemon.

6. *Saké on the rocks*. Pour saké straight over ice cubes. For best results, use undiluted saké (*genshu*) that has been chilled in the refrigerator beforehand.

# The Range of Saké

Like whiskey and beer, saké is produced from a single grain, and the differences between sakés are more subtle than those between wines. Nevertheless, with more than 2,700 brewers in Japan, each adding its own refinements to the traditional art of brewing, saké offers an inexhaustible variety of tasting experiences. Learning to select sakés skillfully is one of the great pleasures of drinking. The first step is to develop an understanding of the types of saké available.

## National Brands and Local Brews

One useful distinction to make is between the national brands, which are available everywhere in Japan, and the local sakés, or *jizake*, which often are available only in the areas where they are produced.

The famous saké-producing regions of Nada near Osaka and of Fushimi near Kyoto have dominated the industry since the late Edo period, and today the fifty largest makers in these two regions account for more than half of Japan's total annual production. In 1981, for example, the twelve largest brands—Gekkeikan, Hakutsuru, Nihonsakari, Shirayuki, Kizakura, Sho-Chiku-Bai, Kiku-Masamune, Hakushika, Sawanotsuru, Kembishi, and Fukumusume—all from Nada or Fushimi, accounted for 39 percent of all saké sold in Japan.

These large makers have also led in the rapid modernization of the industry, introducing new technologies and economies of scale that have helped them consolidate their command of the market.

At the other end of the scale, one can search out the tiny breweries, or kura, that produce only a few thousand bottles of saké a year using traditional techniques and manual labor. A visitor to one of these traditional breweries is transported back to the Edo period: large old wooden tubs swell with steaming rice, workers test the brew with their fingers, the air is ripe with the rich odor of fermentation. Such places, and the thousands of small and medium-size makers scattered all over the country, are the producers of *jizake*, and it is in these local brews that one discovers the full range of saké. The small makers have resisted the domination of the market by the national brands, and they have been rewarded by a recent surge of interest among the Japanese in exploring the possibilities of *jizake* as a sophisticated natural beverage.

Connoisseurs are almost unanimous in contending that the very best sakés are to be found among the local sakés. The large makers may charge that this view is influenced by our nostalgia for the past, our sympathy with the owners of small kura who are stubbornly clinging to the methods of bygone days. This is certainly true. It is also true that some of these small brewers have spent lifetimes attempting to perfect traditional techniques handed down for generations and that, occasionally, one of them produces a saké that truly deserves the name *maboroshi no sake*, "a saké of dreams." The mass-market sakés of the large makers simply do not attain such heights.

A note of caution is needed here. The great advantage of the large makers is that computerized operations and strict standards of quality control make it possible for them to produce sakés that are consistently good, and usually much less expensive than local sakés that have established reputations.

Furthermore, the search for "a saké of dreams" among the local sakés requires considerable knowledge of the industry, and this knowledge must be updated constantly. Any number of factors may affect the quality of sakés produced by local brewers each year. Not the least of these is the danger of success. Once saké critics have discovered an outstanding *jizake* and made it famous, the temptation for the brewer to go commercial is enormous. This almost always requires an expansion of capacity, and a kura owner who succumbs to such temptation soon finds himself making more and more compromises until the unique taste of his saké is finally lost.

A great deal is written about developments in the saké industry by professional saké and food critics, and for those who can read Japanese this provides up-to-date information on outstanding local sakés. People who do not read Japanese—and in fact most Japanese, who simply do not have the time to follow all these developments—can rely on the advice of a trusted liquor store owner and the judgments of the masters of their favorite drinking establishments.

## Types of Saké

As was discussed in Part 1, modernization has led to an increasing exploitation of new techniques of adding alcohol, sugar, cultivated yeast, and other ingredients at various stages in the production process. These new techniques continue to be the subjects of intense debate. Purists insist that saké should be made from rice, kōji rice, and water only, while many brewers contend that the addition of alcohol and other ingredients enables them to respond quickly to changes in consumer tastes and produce excellent sakés at affordable prices. Whatever one's position on this issue, consumers have the right to know what they are buying. In 1975 the Japan Saké Brewers Association finally established self-governing rules for the industry, and these rules were further strengthened in 1982. While still a far cry from the French Appellation Contrôlée system, the labeling standards enforced under the Association system provide a much better idea than before of where the saké comes from, what is in it, and how it was brewed. Common Association and other frequently seen designations are outlined below.

In an important sense, all of the special labeling designations given here describe special types of saké. In addition to the brand name and advertising slogans, the labels on most of the sakés on the market contain only the most obvious kinds of information: the address of the brewer, the date of bottling, the alcohol content, and ingredients. The point is that if the label doesn't mention any of the

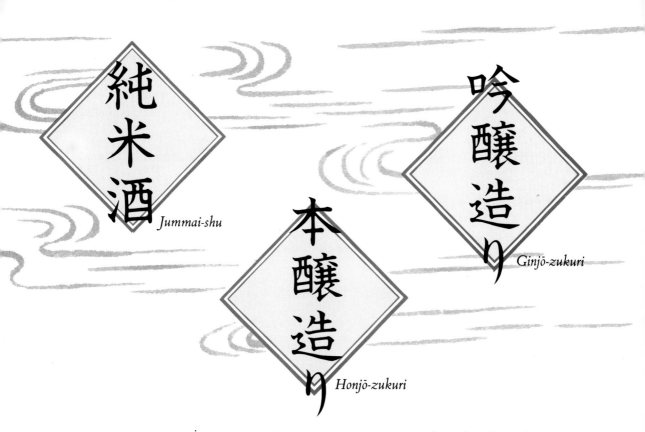

純米酒

*Jummai-shu*

本醸造り

*Honjō-zukuri*

吟醸造り

*Ginjō-zukuri*

special designations the saké is simply an ordinary brew—heightened consumer consciousness has given these designations advertisement value, and brewers will not miss a chance to display them. This is also important because designations are sometimes used together. For example, *jummai taru-zake* is pure rice cask saké, and a saké that is only labeled *taru-zake* is cask saké but almost certainly not pure rice saké.

Because these designations are usually not written in English on the labels, on these pages they appear in both romanized transcription as well as the original Japanese.

### JUMMAI-SHU

This is "pure rice" saké in which only rice, kōji rice, and water are used as ingredients, with no additions of alcohol, sugar, or anything else (water, however, is added at the end to dilute the saké to about 16 percent alcohol). While these sakés have become a special type in the Japanese market, this category is the most important for Americans, because under American tax laws, only "pure rice saké" can be imported. At least in terms of ingredients, *jummai-shu* is closest to the traditional sakés of the Edo period, and it is becoming increasingly popular among young Japanese, many of whom have joined the natural foods movement with a

vengeance. *Jummai-shu* tends to have a heavier taste than most of the Special and First Class sakés produced by the large makers, which usually have added alcohol.

### HONJŌ-ZUKURI [HONJŌ-ZŌ]

Also called *honshikomi* and *hon-zukuri*. In this saké, not more than 120 liters of raw alcohol (100 percent alcohol) per each metric ton of white rice and no glucose have been added during the brewing process. Sakés bearing this designation attempt to preserve the rich taste of sakés produced by traditional techniques while achieving the mildness that is preferred by most Japanese consumers. The Association's regulations stipulate that the raw alcohol must be added to the moromi, where it interacts with and brings out the flavor elements in the mash.

Added alcohol cannot exceed 25 percent of the total alcohol in the finished product.

### GINJŌ-ZUKURI [GINJŌ-ZŌ]

This is a special type of *jummai-shu* or *honjō-zukuri*, and professional tasters are almost unanimous in regarding it as the ultimate achievement of the brewer's art. All the rice employed in brewing *ginjō* sakés must be polished to at least 60 percent of its original size (the kōji rice is polished even further). Additionally,

元酒
*Genshu*

生一本
*Ki-ippon*

たる酒
*Taru-zake*

the normal restrictions on added alcohol apply for *honjō* types. In many *ginjō* sakés brewers use special yeasts—Association No. 9 and No. 10—in making moto, and ferment the final mash very slowly at low temperatures, around 10°C (50°F). The two yeasts used in making these sakés produce a unique tangy flavor and an aroma often compared to that of Delicious apples. They produce relatively small amounts of acid, however, so these sakés are usually light-bodied, with a certain tartness not found in most sakés. Some critics complain that this is a defect and that these sakés tend to taste too sweet. As a result, some brewers of *ginjō* sakés use Association No. 7 yeast, which produces the drier taste that connoisseurs are fond of. Recently, experts at the Tokyo branch of the National Research Institute of Brewing have perfected a new yeast for *ginjō-zukuri* by combining haploids of Association No. 10 and No. 7, the most common saké yeast. This yeast produces the characteristic nose and taste of *ginjō* sakés, but also a higher acidity.

*Ginjō* sakés are only produced in small quantities, and may be difficult to find. They can also be expensive. In 1984 a standard 1.8-liter bottle of Kiku-Masamune's *ginjō* saké, Kohaku, of which only 5,000 bottles were marketed, sold for more than $200. A few *ginjō* sakés are produced with no added alcohol and are marketed in the United States.

## GENSHU

*Genshu* is undiluted saké. After filtration, saké has an alcohol content of around 20 percent. As public tastes have shifted to lighter sakés, most sakés on the market have been diluted with water until their alcohol content falls to between 15 and 17 percent. *Genshu*, with its higher alcohol level and full-bodied taste, is an excellent choice for serving on-the-rocks. *Namazake* 生酒 is a special type of *genshu* that is canned or bottled just as it comes out of the filter from the moromi. It is unpasteurized; the yeast is still active and gives it a zesty, tart flavor. Over time, even when in a sealed container, *namazake* turns yellowish and richens in flavor. *Namazake* must be drunk immediately upon opening. *Genshu* sakés that are also *jummai-shu*—pure rice sakés— are available in the United States.

## TARU-ZAKE

*Taru-zake*, or "cask saké," is aged in wooden casks (18 liters up to 72 liters) so that color, aroma, and flavor elements from the wood are absorbed into the saké. Traditionally, the best wood for the casks is considered to be the Japanese cypress of the Yoshino area of Nara Prefecture. Today *taru-zake* is sold both in casks of various sizes and in glass bottles. As with all sakés, *taru-zake* should be drunk fairly soon after purchase. When it is stored too

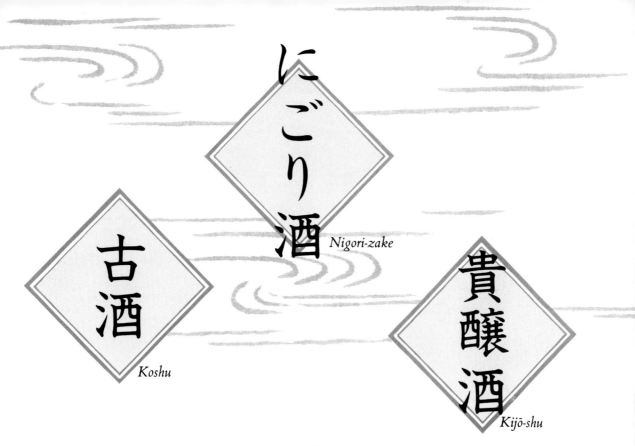

にごり酒
*Nigori-zake*

古酒
*Koshu*

貴醸酒
*Kijō-shu*

long, the flavor of the saké will be overwhelmed by that of the wood. One additional note of a caution should be added concerning the miniature casks of *taru-zake* now on the market. These 1.8-liter "casks" are in fact ceramic bottles that have been decorated to look like traditional wooden *taru*.

## KI-IPPON

Originally, this term was used on labels to indicate that the saké had been produced entirely in a single area and had not been diluted. For example, *Nada no ki-ippon* meant "pure, undiluted saké from Nada." It has new significance today because of the increasingly common practice among large makers of buying saké from subcontractors to blend with the sakés produced in their own factories. A saké labeled with this term has to have been produced entirely by the company that markets it.
Another requirement is that it be *jummai-shu* (pure rice saké). Recently, this term has made a reappearance in Nada. Kiku-Masamune, for example, now markets a saké called Miyabi with the designation *Nada no ki-ippon*.

## KOSHU

Literally "old saké." This saké is aged for two to three years before it is bottled and put on the market. Most sakés are aged for less than one year

before bottling, and should be drunk young. Some high-quality sakés, however, such as *ginjō* sakés, may improve with age, taking on a distinctive mellow flavor. *Hizō-shu* 秘蔵酒 is a special type of *koshu*. Sakés labeled *hizō-shu* must have been aged at least five years before bottling and marketing.

## NIGORI-ZAKE

"Cloudy saké" or "impure saké." This saké is filtered with open-weave sacks that leave some of the solid particles of the rice and kōji rice suspended in the liquid, giving the saké a white, cloudy appearance. *Nigori-zake* resembles home-brewed saké (*doburoku*), which is now illegal. If unpasteurized, the saké may be labeled "active saké" (*kassei seishu* 活性清酒), because the yeast and enzymes in it are still alive and still fermenting. Another saké that looks like *nigori-zake* is produced from sakés that have been filtered in the normal way. Tiny solids sink toward the bottom of the storage tank and form a layer of cloudy saké. Normally, this saké is refiltered, but occasionally it is marketed under the generic term *ori-zake* おり酒.

## KIJŌ-SHU

*Kijō* saké is produced by replacing half of the water used in brewing with saké. It is extremely heavy and sweet, and is usually served as an aperitif.

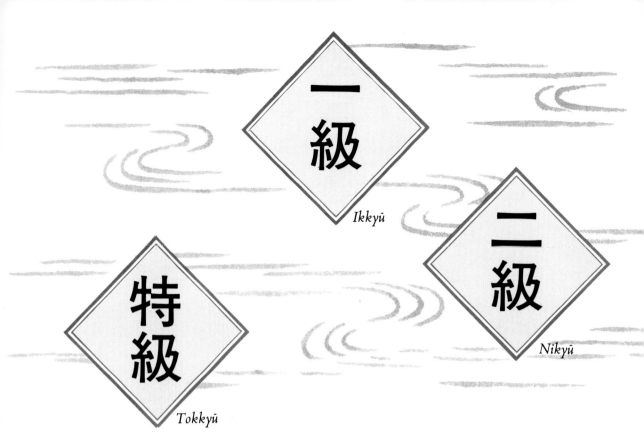

*Ikkyū*

*Nikyū*

*Tokkyū*

### WINE-TYPE SAKÉ

Marketed in Japan as "rice wine," this type of saké is made with the yeast used in grape wines. It has an alcohol content of about 13 percent and a fragrance similar to young white wines. Specialists are also developing a new sherry-type saké by combining haploids of saké yeast and sherry yeast.

### AKAI SAKE AND "NOVELTY SAKÉS"

*Akai sake* is "red saké." Red saké was first produced at the Niigata Prefectural Brewing Experiment Station by using a red-colored kōji instead of the usual yellow type. The color of this saké is indeed bright red, but the flavor is unaffected. It is essentially a sales gimmick, as is the addition of gold flakes or the use of decorative containers. These "novelty" sakés are not particularly distinguished, except that as luxury items they tend to be top-of-the-line brews. Often these are the only forms of certain makers' sakés sold outside of Japan and are worth trying for that reason alone.

## The Official Grades of Saké

The most general classification of sakés is the system of grading administered by the eleven regional offices of the Central Advisory Committee on Alcoholic Beverages. This committee is an organ of the National Tax Ad-

ministration Agency of the Treasury Ministry, which is responsible for regulating the industry as well as for collecting taxes on saké. Under this system, sakés produced in Japan are classified into one of three ranks: *tokkyū* (Special Class), *ikkyū* (First Class), or *nikyū* (Second Class). These classifications are a reliable guide to the relative quality of sakés produced by a single maker, but they can be misleading when used to compare the sakés of different makers, especially in the case of the Second Class grading.

There are two related problems. First is that the system is used not only for grading sakés but also as a basis for taxing them. The tax on a bottle of First Class saké is more than double that on a bottle of Second Class saké, and the tax on Special Class saké is nearly four times as high. The second problem is the ambiguity of the Second Class grading. Each year makers submit sakés they want to have designated as Special or First Class to the office of the Central Advisory Committee in their region. An official chemical analysis, a history, and details of how it was made may accompany each saké sample. Samples are tested individually by reliable teams of tasting experts under carefully controlled conditions. However, a maker may also choose not to submit his saké for testing, in which case it is automatically graded as Second Class. This is a common practice among small brewers who are unwilling, or unable, to pay the higher taxes on the First Class and Special Class grades.

The result is that three different categories of sakés are included in the Second Class grade: (1) sakés intended for Second Class grading to begin with; (2) sakés submitted for First Class grading that fail to pass the tasting test; and (3) sakés not submitted for testing. The last of these three categories includes many outstanding local sakés that would easily pass the tests for First or Special Class grading. Indeed, it is not uncommon for sakés with Second Class grading to be awarded gold medals at tasting concours.

Recent developments have helped reduce confusion among consumers concerning the grading system. The labeling designations described above now provide a reliable guide to distinguishing sakés on the basis of brewing techniques. A saké with *ginjō-zukuri* on its label, even if it is graded Second Class, is almost certainly equal in quality to most sakés labeled Special Class.

The most important thing to remember about the official grading system is that it is a general guide

to the overall quality of sakés submitted for testing. Used together with the labeling system enforced by the Japan Saké Brewers Association, it can be quite useful. Whether produced in a huge automated factory or in a tiny traditional kura, a saké designated as Special Class under the official system must be a "quality saké with distinction," even if the same can be said of many sakés designated as Second Class. Note, however, that a careful reading of labels can often result in the discovery of real bargains among the Second Class—and usually cheaper—sakés.

## Dry Saké and Sweet Saké

One final distinction is between dry sakés (*karakuchi* 辛口) and sweet sakés (*amakuchi* 甘口). The simplest and most readily available guide to dryness and sweetness is called the Nihonshu-do, or saké meter value. This value is a measure of the amount of residual sugar and alcohol in a saké. The saké meter is basically a Baumé meter, which works on the principle that alcohol is lighter than water while glucose is heavier. Water is given a value of $\pm 0$, and a saké with a saké meter value of $\pm 0$ should taste neither particularly dry nor particularly sweet. A positive saké meter value, $+2$ for example, indicates less residual sugar and thus a drier saké. A negative value indicates that the saké will be sweeter. The liquor departments of large department stores usually indicate the saké meter value of sakés on the price tag or with color codes, and most liquor stores can provide saké meter values. How to interpret these values depends to a large extent on the individual, for what is slightly dry to one person may taste neutral or slightly sweet to another. The accompanying figure shows how they are usually interpreted by modern Japanese consumers.

You will get a better idea of how a saké will taste if you can also obtain information about its acidity (mainly the concentration of succinic acid), as this greatly affects dryness and sweetness. The next chart attempts to plot saké meter values and acidity levels to show how they can predict whether a saké will taste dry–heavy, dry–light, sweet–heavy, or sweet–light. Unfortunately, information on acid levels is usually not available to the general consumer. Try contacting the makers directly.

Japanese saké drinkers traditionally prize sakés that are extremely dry and extremely heavy. But preferences have actually undergone a number of radical shifts. Professor Kin'ichirō Sakaguchi has identified one such shift by comparing the average

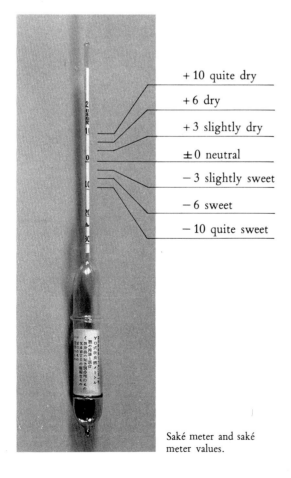

+ 10 quite dry
+ 6 dry
+ 3 slightly dry
± 0 neutral
− 3 slightly sweet
− 6 sweet
− 10 quite sweet

Saké meter and saké meter values.

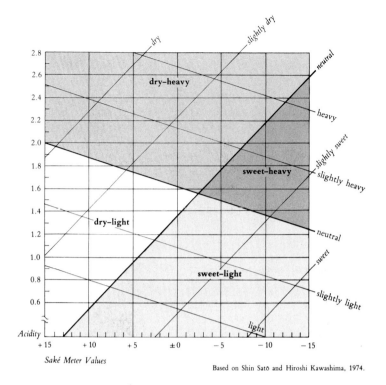

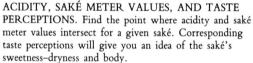

Based on Shin Satō and Hiroshi Kawashima, 1974.

ACIDITY, SAKÉ METER VALUES, AND TASTE
PERCEPTIONS. Find the point where acidity and saké
meter values intersect for a given saké. Corresponding
taste perceptions will give you an idea of the saké's
sweetness–dryness and body.

saké meter values of the top fifty sakés in new saké
contests. From the first new saké contest in 1907
to the sixteenth in 1938, saké meter values dropped
rapidly from + 10.32 to − 10.53. In other words,
in only thirty years, preferences shifted from extremely dry to extremely sweet sakés.

As shown in the next graph a similar radical shift
among Nada sakés occurred in the postwar period,
from dry and heavy to light and sweet types. In
1978, a new pattern began to develop. Preferences
are gradually shifting from sweet to drier sakés,
while the trend toward increasingly lighter sakés
remains strong. In part this reflects the fact that
lighter sakés taste sweeter even if their saké meter
values are higher, but it is also part of a general
trend toward "light" beverages that has influenced
beer and soft drinks as well.

Most connoisseurs prefer dry sakés with substantial body, and many of them express a frank dislike
for sweet sakés. As in selecting wines, however,
the important thing is to find a range of sakés that
you like, and to match individual sakés to the occasion and to the foods served with them.

POSTWAR SHIFTS IN CONSUMER TASTES
(Average Values for Nada Special Class Sakés).

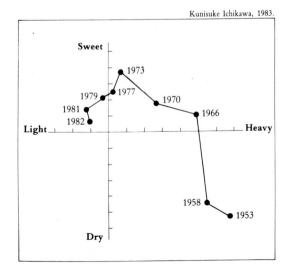

Kunisuke Ichikawa, 1983.

# Saké Tasting

chemical analyses of the sakés. Similar tastings are conducted by the saké companies.

The most enjoyable tastings for professionals occur each year in spring, when brewers invite professional saké critics, distributors, and retailers to their factories or kura to sample the year's new saké. The purpose of such tastings is quite serious. The brewers get an idea of the critical and commercial

Saké-tasting cup with "snake's eye" pattern.

The tradition of saké tasting is almost as old as saké itself. By the Muromachi period, scenes depicting saké tasting show up frequently in Japanese literature and art. It was in the Edo period, however, that brewers and townsmen epicures developed the tasting lexicon that still informs saké connoisseurship today. After the Meiji Restoration of 1868, saké tasters began to borrow the vocabulary of wine tasting from Europeans, and today they often employ such modern terms as volatile acidity, sugar–acid balance, and acetic-acid stink. Anyone familiar with wine, whiskey, or beer tasting will have a substantial head start in approaching saké.

The form saké tasting takes depends on its aim. The regional offices of the Central Advisory Committee on Alcoholic Beverages, for example, conduct official tastings for the purpose of grading sakés, and also sponsor national and regional competitions where prizes are awarded to the outstanding sakés of the year. The official tasters at these events are chosen from government research centers, academia, professional saké critics, and tasters employed by the makers themselves. They must have established reputations for skill and impartiality, and pass a series of extremely difficult tests in order to qualify. The tastings themselves are highly formal, and the results are compared with those of

prospects of their sakés, as well as advice on blending and aging, while the critics and distributors have a chance to make judgments on the sakés they will be recommending to the public. Nevertheless, these tastings have an informal atmosphere and are often followed by a meal, usually lunch, in which one has a chance to enjoy the sakés again, this time with sakana chosen by the brewer himself. In the case of a local saké, this is an opportunity to sample local delicacies selected and prepared by experts.

Most people taste saké (or wine) to discover what they like, and the techniques of professional tasting outlined below need not be followed rigidly in private, informal tastings. They are presented here as a guide to what to look for, and how to find it, when confronted by an unfamiliar saké. Of course, the best way to acquire skill in tasting is to get help from an expert. There is no real substitute for the master taster who will hand you a glass and say, "This is the characteristic nose of

Tasting room at the National Research
Institute of Brewing in Ōji, Tokyo.

*ginjō* saké,'' for once you know what to look for,
it is easy to identify it again. You can approach this
ideal by first sampling a range of sakés recommended
by expert tasters or more experienced friends. Again,
once you know what is good, you can easily tell
if something is wrong. All experts agree that the
most important thing for anyone serious about
tasting is to *drink* saké, and to sample as many different kinds and brands as possible.

## The Tasting Room and Tasting Etiquette

The ideal tasting room is one
with ample natural light, or
lighting designed to approximate natural light, but without
direct exposure to the sun.
North-facing windows provide the most natural
light. Walls should be a light cream color. The
room temperature should be 18°–20°C
(64°–68°F) and the humidity 50–60 percent.
Needless to say, all strong odors are to be avoided:
no smoking in the tasting room, and no strongly
scented perfumes, colognes, or hair sprays.

Saké tasting: determining the nose.

The best time to have a tasting is between ten and eleven o'clock in the morning; the light is best at this hour, and the tasters' taste buds will have recovered from breakfast and still be not quite ready for lunch. At whatever hour a tasting is held, meals should always follow the tasting: it is almost impossible to judge sakés after a large meal.

Sakés are usually served at room temperature—about 20°C (68°F)—for comparative tastings. Occasionally, when the sakés to be compared improve significantly when warmed, they are all brought to a uniform temperature between 40°C (104°F) and 50°C (122°F).

The officially approved saké-tasting cup (*kikizake choko*) used by the Central Advisory Committee on Alcoholic Beverages is a large white porcelain cup with two concentric blue circles on the bottom inside surface. This pattern accounts for its nickname, the "snake's eye cup." The design of the cup plays an important role in tasting. The white part of the pattern provides a perfect background against which to judge the color of the saké, while the "snake's eye" is used to test for transparency (*sae*). The tasting cups are kept about 80 percent full; if a saké is not transparent—if it has a poor *sae*—the line of

contrast between the white and blue of the pattern will be blurry. Occasionally, porcelain cups with a yellow glaze on the inside or glasses with a dark brown tint are employed at some point in the tasting to conceal the color of the sakés. This is to counter a tendency among tasters to be biased in favor of sakés that have less color.

Official tasting cups are produced only for use within the industry, and they are difficult to obtain. But any wide-mouthed, heavy porcelain tea cup with a bold blue-and-white pattern will serve as a good substitute. The miniature snake's eye cups that are quite common in restaurants and drinking places are not good for serious tasting. They are not deep enough to make the transparency test reliable, and are virtually useless in judging smell. Wine-tasting glasses, however, can be perfectly suitable for saké tasting, particularly when tasting sakés that have been aged (*koshu* or *hizō-shu*).

The tasting room is also provided with receptacles for spitting out the saké after tasting, sometimes a large metal can or a barrel filled with newspaper, but usually a small plastic pitcher with a handle that leaves the thumb free to open and close the cover. There is no need to feel self-conscious

Public tasting session at the National Research Institute of Brewing. About 800 *ginjō* sakés from breweries around Japan are rated and then made available for sampling by brewery owners, restaurateurs, and saké vendors.

It gives you a laugh attack.

about spitting. Everyone else will be spitting too,
and while spitting is by no means a breach of tasting
etiquette, getting drunk certainly is. Two more
points: Because the tasting cups are shared, women
should remove their lipstick before tasting begins.
Conversations not having to do with the sakés
should be carried on away from the tasting area.

## How to Taste Saké

As in wine tasting, the basic
sequence when tasting saké
is: look, smell, taste. Note
color and appearance first, scent or bouquet next,
and finally the effect on the palate. A Japanese-style
tasting cup, however, is used somewhat different-
ly from a cup for wine tasting. The following procedure is employed by professional tasters.

### APPEARANCE

Usually, 1.8-liter bottles (*isshō-bin*) of the sakés to
be tasted are lined up with tasting cups in front
of them. Tasting cups are about 80 percent full.
First, lift the cup up and peer straight down into
it. If the contrasting lines between the blue and
white of the snake's-eye pattern are blurred, the
clarity (*sae* or *teri*) of the saké is inferior. This defect
is also referred to as a "white cloudiness" (*shiroboke*).

Next, note the color against the white part of the
cup. Freshly filtered sakés (*namazake*) have a light
lemon color with a tinge of green. The ideal for
young sakés (aged from six months to a year), which
is rarely achieved, is an almost colorless saké with
a green tinge. Ordinary sakés have a light yellow
tint, often described as the color of a Japanese rose
(*yamabuki*), or a light amber hue. Before the advent of activated-charcoal filtering, it was extremely
difficult to achieve perfect clarity and colorlessness,
and these qualities were highly prized. Today,
however, lack of color may be an indication that
activated-charcoal filtering has been overdone, and
the taste of the saké may have disappeared along
with the color. In extreme cases, it will have a
characteristic "charcoal stink." A truly great old
saké, such as the Kidoizumi brewery's Kokin, will
have a slightly green fluorescence. Some old sakés
have an amber hue, which becomes darker as the
saké ages.

### SMELL

Whether it is called aroma, fragrance, bouquet, or
nose, smell is one of the most important elements
in evaluating saké. Saké tasters use more than ninety
words to describe it. After noting the appearance

It fills you with arrogant courage.

It makes you cling to others and bore them with your idiotic chatter.

of the saké, bring the tasting cup closer to your nose and rock the cup gently backward and forward to give the saké air and enable it to "breathe" (the tasting cup will be too full to swirl the saké as one would do with a wine cup). Then smell the "top" of the saké. Finally, lower your nose into the cup to smell the "base" fragrance. It is better to put your nose in several times, noting your impressions, than to leave it there—overexposure dulls the senses. Also, a series of short, gradually deeper sniffs will give a better sense of the smell than one prolonged inhalation. One excellent technique is to inhale the bouquet first through one nostril, then the other, and finally through both. This gives you further opportunities to check first impressions.

### TASTE

Taste is the paramount test of a saké's quality. The technique of tasting saké is almost identical to that of tasting wine. Take a good mouthful and push it all around your mouth. Professional tasters make slurping noises to let in air. This gives the saké more chance to show all its qualities. Another technique is called "biting the saké." Keep your lips tightly closed (to avoid spitting), and make sharp bites with your teeth. This forces the tongue up against the roof of the mouth and the saké into the recesses at the base of the tongue and behind the teeth. After making sure that the saké has reached all the tastebuds, experts then "push the saké into the nose" (*fukumibana*). Make short slurping sounds to suck in air and mix it thoroughly with the saké; then slowly breathe the air out through your nose. The fragrance of the saké in your mouth will fill your nose, giving a much more intense impression

> **NOSE**
>
> *The Japanese for "nose" is* hana, *and this word is often used in tasting terms describing the smell of saké. For example, the following terms describe the rough, unsettled smell of new saké before it is aged ("h" usually changes to a voiced "b" when* hana *is attached to the end of another word):* shinshubana *("new saké nose"),* kōjibana *("a smell of kōji rice"), and* hana ga wakai *("the nose is young"). The nose of a saké that has been aged too long is described by such terms as* koshuka *("old saké stink"),* hineka *("an overripe smell"), and* binka *("bottle stink"). The following words are used to praise a saké that has been aged for just the right length of time and refer to taste and* nodokoshi *(how the saké passes down the throat):* marumi ga aru *("a rounded taste"),* chōwa ga aru *("to have harmony"),* sabake ga yoi *("worldly"),* shitazawari nameraka *("to have a gentle touch on the tongue"), and* suberi ga yoi *("it slips down well").*

of the "nose" and taste of the saké. It is at this stage that the taster comes closest to a total experience of the saké.

Tasters usually spit out the saké after getting a strong impression of its taste, but you will sometimes want to swallow a really fine saké in order to test its *nodokoshi* (how it passes down the throat). The *nodokoshi* should be soft and smooth—"like drinking water." Whether you spit out or swallow, the moments after elimination, when you can note the "finish" or "length of palate" of the saké, are among the most important in tasting, and the ones most often neglected by amateurs. The taste of an excellent saké will linger on the palate. A wine taster would refer to this quality by saying that the saké "has a tail," and this is an almost perfect

It won't let you stop: "Let's go just one more place for another round!"

**INGREDIENTS AND PROCESSES**

*Some terms for nose refer to the characteristic bouquets produced by the various techniques of making moto (yeast mash) or by the Association yeasts used in brewing. The yamahai method of making moto produces a distinctive yamahai bouquet. Each of the Association yeasts has a characteristic nose. Association No. 7, for example, is hanayaka ("lively"), while No. 6 is odayaka ("mild and subdued"). Association No. 9 and No. 10 contribute to ginjōka, the fruity nose and flavor of ginjō sakés. Some modern processes, however, leave a residue that experienced tasters can easily detect. Adding alcohol, glutenous rice, sugar, and other ingredients to the moromi before filtering the saké has given birth to such terms as arukōruka ("alcohol stink"), yakuhinka ("medicine stink"), aminosanka ("amino acid stink"), and yondanka ("fourth addition stink").*

translation of the Japanese tasting terms *shiripin* and *pin*. An ordinary saké will disappear from memory quickly, and a flawed saké will have an unpleasant aftertaste.

TASTING VOCABULARY

The entire procedure outlined above takes only five to six seconds for each saké. Once a saké has been tasted there remains the pleasant task of describing it. The vocabulary of saké tasting is inexhaustible and growing all the time, as tasters create their own words to describe their impressions. It should not be surprising that, in two such traditional arts, the parallels between wine- and saké-tasting terms are numerous. Often it is difficult to tell whether saké tasters borrowed a term from wine tasters or inherited it from their Edo-period predecessors. The three most basic saké tasting terms, *amakuchi*, *karakuchi*, and *shiripin ga aru* (or *pin ga aru*), correspond exactly to "sweet," "dry," and "having a tail." These particular terms were being used in Japan long before the Edo period. The term *sabishii* ("lonely and sad"), which refers to a lack of complexity of taste, belongs to the realm of classical Japanese literature—it describes the mental state of a woman waiting for a lover who fails the rendezvous.

The most basic tasting terms, *amakuchi* and *karakuchi*, can be the most difficult. Acids and other components of the saké can mask residual sugar, so that one saké may taste drier than another even though it has more sugar. This has led to a wide application of the concept of sugar–acid balance,

which is related to a variety of traditional tasting terms that are all related to body: *koku ga aru* ("to have body"), *niku ga aru* ("to have meat"), *haba ga aru* ("to have range"), *fukurami ga aru* ("to have a swell"), and, *nōkōmi* ("a taste of high fermentation"). These terms are all close to the Western tasting term "fat," which implies relatively high acidity and a full-bodied wine, rich in texture and flavor. It does not imply sweetness. The negative counterparts of these terms, formed by changing the Japanese *aru* ("to have") to *nai* ("not to have"), indicate a lack of body (e.g., *koku ga nai*), as does the poetic term *sabishii*.

A different set of terms, mostly adjectives, are used when the saké has too much body: *kudoi* ("garrulous"), *shitsukoi* ("cloying"), *omoi* ("heavy"), *koi* ("thick"), *sabake ga warui* ("unworldly"), and *zatsumi ga aru* ("to have off-flavors"). The last of these refers to the flavors contributed to a saké by tiny particles of rice bran when the rice is not highly polished. Other terms used to describe this quality are *kitanai* ("dirty"), *zarappoi* ("rough"), and *gara ga warui* ("ill-bred"). In general, tasting terms describing defects are more numerous than those of praise.

These tasting terms are the ones most generally used by professional and amateur tasters in Japan. As is true of wine, however, there is no limit to the vocabulary tasters end up using. Nor do your own judgments have to be expressed in Japanese. If you find a word leaping to mind when you smell or taste a saké, use it—as your own contribution to the always-evolving lore of saké.

# Sakés
# for
# the
# Connoisseur

Among all the sakés made in Japan are some that most connoisseurs consider a cut above the rest. There is something about their taste—lucidity, say, or subtlety—that makes them superior expressions of the brewer's ideal. Or it may be something about the particular tradition invested in the brewery, a kind of sureness that renders its brews unmistakably its own.

But drinking is a human sport, and lurking within all saké connoisseurship are broad areas of subjective appraisal. A saké that accompanies a rich venue, a fine meal, or an interesting companion will forever after have attached to it properties unknown to physical chemistry.

And thank goodness for that!

Included in this section are a few sakés that connoisseurs by consensus rate among the best—for whatever reason. It begins with a brief guide to labeling, for there are many occasions when you will be on your own, trying your best to make a connoisseur's choice but perhaps unsure of what to look for.

**How to Read Saké Labels**

Japan's mastery of design in small spaces comes to the fore in the saké label. These miniature works of art can be bold, flowery, traditional, masculine—depending on how the brewer wants his product to be appraised or recognized on the shelf amidst dozens of other, competing brands. While you will be tempted to choose a bottle on the merits of its label design alone, remember that the real virtue of the label for the connoisseur lies in what it tells him about the saké within. The placement of the important clues to taste and quality differs depending on the maker. On page 80, using a bottle of Aramasa saké as a typical example, are some basic things to look for; see also the labels on the following pages. Since most saké labels will be written in Japanese, refer to the preceding discussion on types of saké for Japanese terms, or ask a friend to accompany you to the liquor store. Labels on sakés intended for export usually contain less information—and are often written in English.

## NECK

"KŌKYŪ SEISHU." "High-class pure saké." Merely a slogan.

"HONJŌ-ZUKURI" Important. This tells you that the saké contains added alcohol, but no more than 120 liters to each ton of polished rice. See page 67.

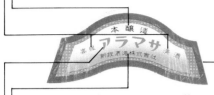

"ARAMASA SHUZŌ KABUSHIKIGAISHA." The name of the brewer: "Aramasa Brewery Corporation."

"ARAMASA." The brand name, written in *katakana*, an angular phonetic script.

## ASSOCIATION LABELS

Since 1975 the Japan Saké Brewers Association has been providing member brewers with standardized labels to indicate the official grades and ingredients of their sakés. Not all brewers belong to the Association, so you will sometimes see labels which display similar information but which differ in shape and color. In the ingredients listings, and this is useful to know if you don't want to bother with deciphering the Japanese, the presence of two items almost always indicates that the saké is *jummai-shu*, or pure rice saké. Three items indicate that alcohol has been added, while four items indicate that brewer's sugar has also been used. The second of the three labels shown here is from the bottle of Aramasa.

"TOKKYŪ." Special Class.

PERCENTAGE OF ALCOHOL. 15 to 16 percent.

"KOME, KOME KŌJI." Rice and kōji rice are the ingredients. This is *jummai-shu*. Water is not listed as an ingredient.

"IKKYŪ." First Class.

"KOME, KOME KŌJI, JŌZŌYŌ ARUKŌRU." Rice, kōji rice, and brewer's alcohol.

"NIKYŪ." Second Class.

"KOME, KOME KŌJI, JŌZŌYŌ ARUKŌRU, JOZŌYŌ TŌRUI." Rice, kōji rice, brewer's alcohol, brewer's sugar.

## BODY

The content of the main label on the body of the bottle has no set formula. Usually, if a sake is *jummai-shu* or *honjō-zukuri*, the label will say so. You will often see the terms *karakuchi* and *amakuchi*, indicating dryness and sweetness, respectively. Information may be hard to identify, however, owing to the variety of written scripts used and the presence of slogans and promotional blurbs.

STATEMENT OF REGISTRY.

"ARAMASA." The name of the brewer appears here in ideograms and in the same angular phonetic script ("A-ra-ma-sa") used on the neck.

"MEISEI KAN SHIKAI." Roughly, "Known for its excellence throughout the world." The script reads vertically from right to left.

"HONJŌ-ZUKURI SEISHU." Important. This tells you the saké is *honjō-zukuri*, as was also noted on the neck. The script is in a style used on official seals.

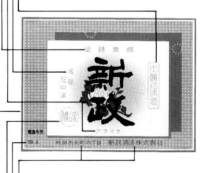

"59.6." Here's what to look for—the date of bottling: "June of the 59th year." In Japan, years are counted from the beginning of an emperor's reign. Since the reign of the present emperor began in 1926, the 59th year is 1984; 1985 will be the 60th year, and so on. The same dating system is also used for some saké bottles imported into the United States.

"KINJŌ." The script here reads from right to left: "Brewed with devotion."

THE NAME AND ADDRESS OF THE BREWERY.

Aramasa.

Gokyo.

Hira Izumi.

Eisen.

Goshun.

Hitorimusume.

Fukumasamune.

Gozenshu.

Ichinokura.

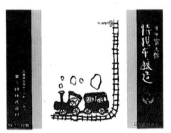

Fukunishiki.

Hatsumago.

Iwanoi.

Kamikokoro.

Koshinohomare.

Madonoume.

Kidoizumi.

Koshinokambai.

Masumi.

Kikuhime.

Kotsuzumi.

Meibou.

Kikunoshiro.

Momokawa.

Koro.

Kusudama.

Nanawarai.

Nishinoseki.

Suishin.

Tsukinokatsura.

Otokoyama.

Taruhei.

Umenishiki.

Ōyama.

Tateyama.

Urakasumi.

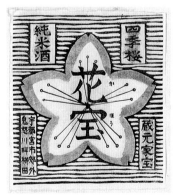

Shikizakura.

Toyonoaki.

Wakaebisu.

Tsukasabotan.

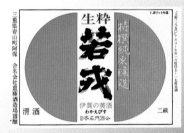

Wakatake Onikoroshi.

Chiyoda.

Haku-taka.

Ozeki.

Fuju.

Hakutsuru.

Sakura-Masamune.

Fu-ki.

Ichidai.

Sawanotsuru.

Gekkeikan.

Kamotsuru.

Sempuku.

Genji.

Kiku-Masamune.

Shirayuki.

Hakushika.

Nihonsakari.

Sho-Chiku-Bai.

## 40 Good Sakés: A Selection

On this page and the following two pages are descriptions of the sakés whose labels appear in color on pages 81–83. Each saké is listed by its brand name; in some cases a second name is given to distinguish the saké from other sakés by the same maker. Saké meter values (SMV) and acidity levels can be used with the graph on page 72 as a rough guide to taste; these figures will vary slightly from year to year. More information on the foods mentioned in the taster's comments appears below in the section "Food with Saké: Sakana." Many of these premium sakés are *jizake*, local brews, and their availability in large cities in Japan is usually restricted to selected liquor shops and drinking establishments. Contact the makers (by letter or by phone, in Japanese if possible) for information about suppliers. For descriptions of high-quality sakés available in the United States, see page 89.

### ARAMASA

*Jummai-shu*, Second Class
SMV: +3, Acidity: 1.5

The representative dry saké from Akita Prefecture, where sakés tend to be sweet. Wonderful nose. The kura is known for its discovery of Association No. 6 yeast. Best at room temperature. ARAMASA SHUZŌ CO., Ō-MACHI 6-2-35, AKITA-SHI, AKITA 010

### EISEN: TOKUJŌ

*Honjō-zukuri*, Special Class
SMV: −1, Acidity: 1.4

Rice used is Toyonishiki, polished 70 percent. Neither dry nor sweet, this saké's fine balance of flavors keeps one from getting bored with it. Best warmed. EISEN SHUZŌ CO., EKIMAE-MACHI 2-1, AIZU WAKAMATSU-SHI, FUKUSHIMA 965

### FUKUMASAMUNE: KURO'OBI

*Honjō-zukuri*, First Class
SMV: +2, Acidity: 1.6

Fukumasamune's regular saké is sweet, but Kuro'obi is dry and full-bodied. Aged two years before marketing. Good either at room temperature or warm. FUKUMITSUYA CO., ISHIBIKI-MACHI 2-8-3, KANAZAWA-SHI, ISHIKAWA 920

### FUKUNISHIKI

*Honjō-zukuri*, Second Class
SMV: −1, Acidity: 1.6

Produced in Hyōgo Prefecture, but not a typical Nada saké. A bit dry tasting, with a long nose and palate. Best at room temperature or slightly warm. Overheating will ruin it.

FUKUNISHIKI CO., MIKUCHI-CHŌ 1048, KASAI-SHI, HYŌGO 675-22

### GOKYO: TOKUSEN

*Honjō-zukuri*, First Class
SMV: −1, Acidity: 1.4

Slightly sweet, refreshing, light on the palate, and exceptionally clean. Good either at room temperature or warm. Best with light sakana. SAKAI SHUZŌ CO., NAKAZU-MACHI 1-1-31, IWAKUNI-SHI, YAMAGUCHI 740

### GOSHUN

*Honjō-zukuri*, First Class
SMV: −1, Acidity: 1.4

The representative brew of Ikeda, historically a famous saké-producing area. Good bouquet, strong body, and well balanced. Goes down very smoothly. First sip is elegantly sweet. Best at room temperature. Wonderful with *sashimi*. GOSHUN CO., AYAHA 1-2-2, IKEDA-SHI, OSAKA 563

### GOZENSHU

*Jummai-shu*, Second Class
SMV: ±0, Acidity: 1.7

Smooth, highly drinkable. Slightly dry and very refreshing. Best at room temperature. Excellent with seafood. Gozenshu also makes an ultra-dry (+12 ～ +17) saké with an alcohol content of 30 percent. TSUJI HONTEN CO., KATSUYAMA 116, KATSUYAMA-CHŌ, MANIWA-GUN, OKAYAMA 717

### HATSUMAGO

*Honjō-zukuri*, First Class
SMV: −2, Acidity: 1.6

A dry saké that somehow doesn't seem dry. Very distinctive taste; some

people don't like it. Made with traditional raw moto method. Name means "first grandchild"; the kura says that, like a first grandchild, it will be loved by everyone. Best at room temperature. TŌHOKU MEIJŌ CO., HON-CHŌ 3-10, SAKATA-SHI, YAMAGATA 998

### HIRA IZUMI

*Honjō-zukuri*, First Class
SMV: ±0, Acidity: 1.4

Dry with a strong nose, full body, and highly complex taste. Brewed with the *yamahai* moto method. Good either at room temperature or warm. Goes well with white fish and with shrimp and other shellfish. HIRA IZUMI HOMPO CO., AZA NAKA-MACHI 59, HIRA-SAWA, NIKAHO-MACHI, YURI-GUN, AKI-TA 018-04

### HITORIMUSUME: SAYAKA

*Honjō-zukuri*, Second Class
SMV: +10, Acidity: 1.5

Very refreshing and does not taste as dry as its saké meter value would suggest. Light on the palate and goes down smoothly. Representative of the dry, light sakés that are gaining in popularity among young people. Best at room temperature. Excellent with *tempura* and other deep-fried dishes. Ideal for people who usually drink whiskey or other spirits. YAMANAKA SHUZŌ CO., SHIN-ISHIGE 187, ISHIGE-MA-CHI, YŪKI-GUN, IBARAKI 300-27

### ICHINOKURA: TOKUSEN

*Honjō-zukuri*, Second Class
SMV: +3.5, Acidity: 1.5

Highly refreshing, light, and very popular. The kura has expanded as a result. Best chilled to 12°–13°C

(53°–55°F). Excellent with seafood, especially with the specialty of the Sendai region where it is brewed: *sasakamaboko*, a fishcake served with soy sauce and horseradish. ICHINOKURA CO., AZA ŌKEYAKI 14, SENGOKU, MATSUYAMA-SHI, SHIDA-GUN, MIYAGI 987-13

## IWANOI: DAIGINJŌ

*Honjō-zukuri*, Second Class
SMV: +5, Acidity: 1.2

Rice used is Yamadanishiki, polished 50 percent. A rare "saké of dreams." Very dry, but with low acidity and mellow taste. Best at room temperature. Excellent with seafood such as abalone and lobster. IWASE SHUZŌ CO., KUBO 1916, ONJUKU-MACHI, ISUMI-GUN, CHIBA 299-51

## KAMIKOKORO: HIHŌ

*Honjō-zukuri*, Second Class
SMV: −6, Acidity: 1.35

The kura uses refrigeration equipment to retard fermentation during brewing, so the sweetness suggested by its saké meter value does not appear on the surface or cloy the palate. Extremely subtle, with a refined, delicate taste. One of the best of the diminishing number of good sweet sakés. Good either at room temperature or warm. KAMIKOKORO SHUZŌ CO., YORISHIMA-CHŌ 7500-2, ASAKUCHI-GUN, OKAYAMA 714-01

## KIDOIZUMI

*Honjō-zukuri*, Second Class
SMV: +3 ~ +10, Acidity: 1.6

Yeast mash is made with the traditional *yamahai* moto method. Light and dry with a rich, complex flavor. Serve at room temperature or warm. Excellent with light seafood. The kura also produces a *koshu* called A.L.P.S., which is excellent as an aperitif, and a true "saké of dreams," Kokin, which is aged ten years. KIDOIZUMI SHUZŌ CO., ŌHARA 7635-1, ŌHARA-MACHI, ISUMI-GUN, CHIBA 298

## KIKUHIME: YAMAHAI JUMMAI-SHU

*Jummai-shu*, Second Class
SMV: ±0, Acidity: 2.1

Brewed with the *yamahai* moto method. Full-bodied but refined and very refreshing. Has won many gold and silver medals at national saké-tasting conventions and is widely known. Serve at room temperature, warm, or on the rocks. Its high acidity goes well with deep-fried and other heavy dishes. KIKUHIME GŌSHI LTD., SHIN-MACHI, TSURUGI-MACHI, ISHIKAWA-GUN, ISHIKAWA 920-21

## KIKUNOSHIRO

*Honjō-zukuri*, Second Class
SMV: −2 ~ −3, Acidity: 1.5

Takes full advantage of Association No. 9 yeast. Slightly sweet and very refined. The kura's annual output is very small and includes an extremely full-bodied *ginjo* saké with a saké meter value of +2.5. KIKUNOSHIRO HOMPO CO., ŌAZA WAIFU 95, KIKUCHI-SHI, KUMAMOTO 861-13

## KORO: DAIGINJŌ

*Honjō-zukuri*, Second Class
SMV: +3.5, Acidity: 1.3

A representative *ginjo* saké. Does not taste as dry as its saké meter value would suggest. Drink at room temperature or warm it in a brandy glass with your hands: the nose is superb. KUMAMOTO-KEN SHUZŌ KENKYŪSHO CO., SHIMASAKI 1-7-20, KUMAMOTO-SHI, KUMAMOTO 860

## KOSHINOHOMARE

*Jummai-shu*, First Class
SMV: +5, Acidity: 1.8

Made with rice from Niigata Prefecture. Dry, but aging for two years gives it a mellow flavor. Best at room temperature or slightly warm. Its high acidity complements meat and other relatively heavy sakana. HARA SHUZŌ CO., SHIMBASHI 5-12, KASHIWAZAKI-SHI, NIIGATA 945

## KOSHINOKAMBAI

*Honjō-zukuri*, First Class
SMV: +5, Acidity: 1.4–1.5

The saké that launched the *jizake* boom. Connoisseurs consider it a "saké of dreams." Light and dry, excellent either at room temperature or warm. Good with cold-water fish and other seafood. ISHIMOTO SHUZŌ CO., KITAYAMA 847-1, NIIGATA-SHI, NIIGATA 950-01

## KOTSUZUMI

*Jummai-shu*, First Class
SMV: −1.5, Acidity: 1.6

Brewed from famous local rice called Fukunohana. Beautiful and refined, with body and complex taste. Goes down very smoothly. Best at room temperature. NISHIYAMA SHUZŌJŌ LTD., NAKA TAKEDA 1171, ICHIJIMA-MACHI, HIKAMI-GUN, HYŌGO 669-43

## KUSUDAMA

*Honjō-zukuri*, Second Class
SMV: +3, Acidity: 1.8

Dry and highly distinctive. Full-bodied, but has a certain casualness and goes down very smoothly. Good either at room temperature or warm. Local mountain vegetables make the best sakana. HIRASE SHUZŌTEN LTD., KAMI ICHINO-MACHI 811, TAKAYAMA-SHI, GIFU 506

## MADONOUME

*Honjō-zukuri*, First Class
SMV: +3, Acidity: 1.5

Very nice on the palate, refreshing and dry with good body. Excellent either at room temperature or warm. MADONOUME SHUZŌ CO., ŌAZA SHINDEN 1833, KUBOTA-MACHI, SAGA-GUN, SAGA 849-02

## MASUMI

*Honjō-zukuri*, Second Class
SMV: +1, Acidity: 1.5

Association No. 7 yeast was discovered at this kura. Refreshing and light with a wonderful tail. Never boring. Serve either at room temperature or warm. MIYASAKA JŌZŌ CO., MOTO-MACHI 1-16, SUWA-SHI, NAGANO 392

## MEIBOU

*Jummai-shu*, First Class
SMV: +1.5, Acidity: 1.4–1.5

Very drinkable with a wide range of tastes. Slightly dry, light and easy on the palate. Best chilled or at room temperature. SHIBATA LTD., SHINANO-CHŌ 4-88, SETO-SHI, AICHI 480-12

## MOMOKAWA: DAIGINJŌ

*Honjō-zukuri*, Special Class
SMV: +5, Acidity: 1.3

Brewed from Yamadanishiki rice. Representative of the highly refined *jizake* from northeastern Japan. Exceedingly elegant taste. Serve at room temperature or chilled to about 8°C (46°F). Complements light sakana, particularly local specialities like simmering tofu. NIHOKU SHUZŌ CO., KAMI AKEDŌ 112, MOMOISHI-MACHI, KAMI-KITA-GUN, AOMORI 039-22

## NANAWARAI

*Honjō-zukuri*, First Class
SMV: − 1, Acidity: 1.3

Slightly dry; soft and mild with very light taste. Best at room temperature or slightly warm. Excellent with mountain vegetables and pickled foods. NANAWARAI SHUZŌ CO., KISO FUKUSHIMA-MACHI 5135, KISO-GUN, NAGANO 397

## NISHINOSEKI: TEZUKURI

*Honjō-zukuri*, First Class
SMV: − 2, Acidity: 1.5

Very mild with a savory bouquet and surprisingly complex aftertaste. Drink either warm or at room temperature. Brewery also produces a *ginjō*, Bigin (SMV: + 2, acidity: 1.4), that is excellent warm. KAYAJIMA SHUZŌ CO., TSUNAI 392-1, KUNISAKI-MACHI, HIGASHI KUNISAKI-GUN,ŌITA 873-32

## OTOKOYAMA: KIMOTO

*Jummai-shu*, Second Class
SMV: + 4, Acidity: 1.6

One of Japan's most famous sakés. Brewery uses raw moto method with its own cultivated yeast. Extremely dry and full-bodied saké with "traditional" appeal. Serve at room temperature or warm. Best with *sashimi* and other light sakana. OTOKOYAMA CO., NAGAYAMA NIJŌ 7-64-1, ASAHIKAWA-SHI, HOKKAIDO 078-02

## ŌYAMA

*Jummai-shu*, Second Class
SMV: + 3, Acidity: 1.45

Excellent dry saké. Full-bodied but refreshing with superb nose. Best at room temperature; warming may damage its bouquet. Good with white-fleshed *sashimi* and other light dishes. KATŌ KAHACHIRŌ SHUZŌ CO., ŌYAMA 3-1-38, TSURUOKA-SHI, YAMAGATA 997-11

## SHIKIZAKURA: KAHŌ

*Jummai-shu*, Special Class
SMV: ± 0, Acidity: 1.2

Truly outstanding. It spreads over the palate and unfolds in a symphony of flavors. The kura grows all its own rice and also produces a *daiginjō* ("grand" *ginjō*), Hijiri, one of Japan's "saké of dreams." Hijiri is extremely difficult to obtain, with waiting lists for each year's supply. UTSUNOMIYA SHUZŌ CO., YANAGIDA-MACHI 248, UTSUNOMIYA-SHI, TOCHIGI 321

## SUISHIN

*Jummai-shu*, Second Class
SMV: − 2, Acidity: 1.8

Slightly dry, despite the low saké meter value—note the acidity scale. The famous artist and saké connoisseur Taikan Yokoyama drank a 1.8-liter bottle of this saké every day even in his seventies. SUISHIN YAMANE HONTEN CO., HIGASHI-MACHI 353-2, MIHARA-SHI, HIROSHIMA 723

## TARUHEI

*Jummai-shu*, First Class
SMV: + 1, Acidity: 2

"Handmade" saké. Aging in cedar casks for a week before bottling produces a superb balance between the saké and wood flavors. Highly individual, with many fans, among them the famous writer Hisashi Inoue. Serve at room temperature or lukewarm. Overheating spoils the nose. TARUHEI SHUZŌ CO., NAKAKOMATSU 2886, KAWANISHI-MACHI, HIGASHI OKITAMA-GUN, YAMAGATA 999-01

## TATEYAMA

*Honjō-zukuri*, First Class
SMV: + 3, Acidity: 1.3

Light and dry, easy to drink. Best chilled or at room temperature. Good with a wide range of sakana. TATEYAMA SHUZŌ CO., NAKANO 220, TONAMI-SHI, TOYAMA 939-13

## TOYONOAKI

*Jummai-shu*, First Class
SMV: − 2, Acidity: 1.5

Light and slightly sweet with very highbred taste. Serve at room temperature or warm. Goes well with a wide range of sakana, including raw seafood and *teriyaki*. YONEDA SHUZŌ CO., HIGASHI HON-MACHI 3-59, MATSUE-SHI, SHIMANE 690

## TSUKASABOTAN

*Jummai-shu*, Second Class
SMV: ± 0, Acidity: 1.6

Dry tasting and very drinkable, loved by the famous drinkers of the Tosa region of Shikoku. The "tail" disappears quickly, but is well worth savoring. Serve at room temperature. Best with the Tosa speciality *katsuo tataki*, quick-seared slices of raw bonito with soy sauce and grated ginger. TSUKASABOTAN SHUZŌ CO., SAKAWA-MACHI, TAKAOKA-GUN, KŌCHI 789-12

## TSUKINOKATSURA: TOKUSEN

*Honjō-zukuri*, Second Class
SMV: + 3, Acidity: 1.7

Dry, with characteristic nose of *ginjō* sakés. Best at room temperature. Serve with light dishes. The same kura also produces a very fine *nigori-zake*. MASUDA TOKUBEI SHŌTEN CO., SHIMO-TOBA 24, OSADA-CHŌ, FUSHIMI-KU, KYOTO 612

## UMENISHIKI

*Honjō-zukuri*, First Class
SMV: − 1.5, Acidity: 1.6

Light, with characteristic nose of *ginjō* sakés and refreshing, highly refined flavor. The kura has expanded rapidly as a result of the *jizake* boom. Excellent at room temperature or warm. YAMAKAWA SHUZŌ CO., KANAGAWA 14, KANADA-MACHI, KAWANOE-SHI, EHIME 799-01

## URAKASUMI

*Jummai-shu*, First Class
SMV: − 1, Acidity: 1.3

Another saké that helped lead the boom in *jizake* and *ginjō* saké. Delicate, dry, and very well balanced, with excellent nose and exceptionally complex taste. Serve at room temperature. Good with *sashimi* or raw oysters. SAURA CO., MOTO-MACHI 2-19, SHIOGA-MA-SHI, MIYAGI 985

## WAKAEBISU

*Jummai-shu*, Second Class
SMV: ± 0, Acidity: 1.5

Light and casual, superficially simple but mysteriously subtle. Excellent either at room temperature or warm. Drink with seafood and other light dishes. SHIGEFUJI SHUZŌJŌ LTD., AO 1317, AOYAMA-CHŌ, NAGA-GUN, MIE 518-02

## WAKATAKE ONIKOROSHI (ONIKOROSHI WAKATAKE)

*Honjō-zukuri*, Second Class
SMV: + 9, Acidity: 1.3

Many sakés are given the name *onikoroshi* ("demon slayer"), but this stands at the top. Strong nose and full-bodied. Extremely dry. Serve at room temperature or on the rocks. ŌMURAYA SHUZŌJŌ CO., HONDŌRI 1-8129, SHIMADA-SHI, SHIZUOKA 427

Label for Takara Musume, from Hawaii.

Label for Ozeki, brewed in the United States.

Label for the Takara brewery's American brand, Sho Chiku Bai.

Drinking saké at Renge, a Japanese restaurant in New York City.

## Saké in the United States

With the recent proliferation of Japanese restaurants in major cities throughout the United States, more and more Americans are being exposed to saké for the first time. But there are several obstacles that must be overcome before saké catches on with Americans as wine has. The range of sakés in liquor stores is limited, and distribution is spotty. Americans still do not know enough about saké to make well-informed judgments, and they tend to associate the beverage with dainty cups and high-priced Japanese restaurants. They too frequently drink it overheated and thus never experience its true flavor and aroma.

Saké makers in Japan are working to make their product more accessible to American, and modern Japanese, tastes. In addition to lightening their brews, they are also developing such concoctions as saké cocktails, barbarisms to the connoisseur, perhaps, but pleasantly drinkable all the same. A few saké cocktail recipes appear in this book on page 64. By law all sakés imported into the United States must be *jummai-shu*, pure rice saké, with no added alcohol or sugar. When selecting sakés in a store, however, be sure to check the production date on the label: much time may have passed in warehousing and shipping before the bottle reached the shelf, and it may then have sat there for a considerable

while before you wandered in. Don't buy anything over a year old, and if more than seven or eight months have passed, drink the saké immediately after purchase.

Pure rice saké is also being made in the United States, currently by three companies. The Honolulu Sake Brewing and Ice Company was founded in 1908 in Hawaii as the first saké brewery outside Japan and produces Takara Masamune and Takara Musume sakés (SMV: + 1, acidity: 1.7). Ozeki San Benito, founded in 1979 in Hollister, California, is partly owned by the Ōzeki brewery of Nishinomiya and makes Ozeki (SMV: ±0, acidity: 1.7). Takara Sake USA, established by the Takara brewery of Fushimi in 1982 on the site of a saké brewery formerly belonging to Nomura Sake, makes Sho Chiku Bai (SMV: − 1.0 ~ − 1.5, acidity: 1.9–2.0). These makers all use American-grown short-grain rice and traditional brewing methods. Their sakés are not available in Japan; for American distributors of these and Japanese export sakés, see page 125.

Japanese export sakés are mostly the product of the large Nada and Fushimi makers. Being pure rice sakés, these are all top-class brands, even if they do hover somewhere near the average in terms of taste. Recently, however, Meimonshukai, a distributor of *jizake* in Japan, has been making some of these more idiosyncratic local brews available to American saké fanciers through Restaurant Nippon in New York City (145 E. 52nd Street). Among the sakés you can sample there are Aramasa, Ōyama, Fukunishiki, Hitorimusume, Ichinokura, and Tsukasabotan (see pages 85–87). From spring of 1985, the company is planning on extending its outlets to Chicago, Los Angeles, and San Francisco. If there is sufficient consumer demand, one can expect that it is only a matter of time before Americans will be able to pick and choose from sakés that reflect the full range of Japan's traditional brewing art.

## Japanese Export Sakés

The descriptions on this page refer to the sakés whose labels appear in color on page 84. All these sakés are currently being exported to the United States. The distributors listed on page 125 can give you more information. American laws restrict the use of additives in imported alcoholic beverages. The sakés here, therefore, are all *jummai-shu*, pure rice sakés; brews of the same name but available in Japan may contain added alcohol—check the labels. Class designations, which do not apply in the United States, have been omitted.

---

### CHIYODA

SMV: −1, Acidity: 1.8

Produced by the Midorikawa brewery of Niigata for Suntory Ltd., which markets it only in the United States. Light and drinkable saké aimed at American tastes.

### FUJU

SMV: +3, Acidity: 1.6

From Nada. Slightly dry tasting. Brewed by hand with traditional raw moto technique.

### FU-KI

SMV: −1, Acidity: 1.6

One of Nada's most popular brands. Light tasting and neutral, extremely easy to drink.

### GEKKEIKAN

SMV: ±0, Acidity: 1.6

Full-bodied, with an extremely rich nose. The brewery was established in 1637 and is one of the representative saké makers of Fushimi, producing 108 million liters a year and exporting to sixty-seven countries.

### GENJI

SMV: +1.5, Acidity: 1.5

A *jizake* from Shizuoka Prefecture. Light and very drinkable.

### HAKUSHIKA

Special—SMV: ±0, Acidity: 1.8
Deluxe—SMV: ±0, Acidity: 1.7

Founded in 1662, the brewery is one of the representative saké makers of Nishinomiya. Uses many traditional techniques and produces 33 million liters per year. Widely available.

### HAKU-TAKA

SMV: −1.5, Acidity: 1.6–1.7

From Nishinomiya. Slightly dry and full-bodied, with a long tail worth savoring.

### HAKUTSURU

SMV: +1.8, Acidity: 1.7

From Nada. Light, with a complex nose and palate, but extremely clean. The brewery produces 70 million liters a year.

### ICHIDAI

SMV: −1 ~ ±0, Acidity: 2.0–2.1

From Hiroshima. Dry with a very delicate taste. Ichidai was the first brewer to introduce paper cartons as saké containers.

### KAMOTSURU

SMV: ±0 ~ +1, Acidity: 1.3

From Hiroshima. Well balanced and slightly dry with extremely complex taste that preserves classical ideals of excellence.

### KIKU-MASAMUNE

SMV: +3, Acidity: 1.7

From Nada. Made with raw moto method and other traditional techniques. Brewery is representative of the so-called Nada flavor. Its *ki-ippon* saké, Miyabi, is truly outstanding. Annual production 38 million liters.

### NIHONSAKARI

SMV: −4, Acidity: 2

From Nishinomiya. The brewery makes both sweet and dry sakés, with the export *jummai-shu* being slightly sweet. Annual production 70 million liters.

### OZEKI

SMV: ±0, Acidity: 1.9–2.0

From Nada. Extremely light and drinkable. Founded in 1711, Ōzeki is one of the famous Nada brewers. Ozeki San Benito, which brews saké in California, is a subsidiary.

### SAKURA-MASAMUNE

SMV: +0.5, Acidity: 2

From Nada. Full-bodied and sweet, with a unique palate and nose. Tazaemon, the sixth owner of the brewery, is the legendary pioneer of Nada saké, responsible for the discovery of *miyamizu* (Nishinomiya water) and new techniques of polishing rice.

### SAWANOTSURU

*Genshu*—SMV: 2, Acidity: 1.9, Alcohol Percentage: 18.7
*Jummai-shu*—SMV: −2, Acidity: 1.7–1.9

From Nada. The *jummai-shu* is light and dry, with a rich taste of rice. Excellent with Chinese cuisine. Annual production 31 million liters.

### SEMPUKU

SMV: −2, Acidity: 1.6

A *jizake* from Hiroshima. Complex and full-bodied. Excellent warmed.

### SHIRAYUKI

SMV: +1, Acidity: 2.1

Highly complex palate and nose. Much loved by connoisseurs. Konishi Shuzō is one of the representative brewers of the Itami region. Annual production 33 million liters.

### SHO-CHIKU-BAI

Deluxe—SMV: −1.5, Acidity: 1.9
Regular—SMV: −1.5, Acidity: 1.8

Dry, very well balanced. Takara Shuzō is one of the representative brewers of Fushimi. Annual production 39 million liters. Takara Sake, which brews saké in the United States, is a subsidiary.

# *A Drinker's Guide*

Now that you are familiar with the kinds of saké and the words you can use to display your newly found connoisseurship, the next step is to find some brew and drink it. The section that follows presents orthodox approaches, only because these are probably what you will find in Japan. But how you entertain in your own home is another matter, and whether you serve saké with traditional Japanese food or with pizza and a tossed salad is up to you. Brewers themselves have been experimenting with new ways of enjoying saké in the hope of broadening their market, and in addition to cocktails there are now carbonated sakés, wine-type sakés, and sakés in chill-packs and a variety of other convenient-sized bottles and paper containers.

**Warming Saké** Almost everyone knows that saké is served warm in small pitchers (called *tokkuri* or *o-chōshi*), and that it is drunk from tiny cups (*sakazuki* or *o-choko*). In fact, this is only one of many ways to drink saké. How it should be served on a particular occasion will depend on the setting, the season, the cuisine, the type and quality of the saké itself, and individual taste.

Many connoisseurs insist that warming saké distorts its true taste, and few people would warm a truly outstanding saké. Heating a mediocre saké will only emphasize its defects. But there are some occasions when saké is best warm. A dry saké drunk warm, for example, will reveal its distinctive nose and flavor. And in the Edo period, the favorite dictum of connoisseurs was: "The saké should be warm, the cuisine *sashimi*, and the pourer a beautiful woman."

Remember, however, that "warm" does not mean "hot." The most common complaint of saké brewers is that people overheat their saké, and their most vehement comments are reserved for Americans: "Americans like their beer icy and their coffee boiling—unfortunately, they treat saké like coffee." This is worth bearing in mind, both when you serve saké at home and when you go out. All sakés available in the United States are *jummai-shu*, pure rice sakés, which are apt to become syrupy and cloying if allowed to cool after being warmed too much. Overheating also causes the alcohol and taste elements to evaporate, leaving you with an impotent brew. You have two ways of avoiding this. One is to drink saké at room temperature (*hiya*), on the rocks, or in cocktails. The other is to learn something about warming saké yourself.

There are many methods of warming saké. Restaurants often use saké-warming machines, and small electric saké warmers are available for home use. These devices are almost always useless because they are imprecise. The best method, and the easiest to use at home, is still the old-fashioned one of warming a tokkuri in a pan of hot water. Simple as it may sound, this method requires a modicum of skill. Many people make the mistake of putting the tokkuri in a pan of cold water and then heating the water and the saké together. This almost always results in overheating: by the time the water has begun to simmer, so has the saké. Starting with boiling water is also no good. The water in the warming pan should be kept at a steady temperature just below a simmer, so that the saké warms gradually.

The hard part begins after you put the tokkuri in the water. Ideal temperatures for the various degrees of warming can be specified, but one hardly wants to pop a thermometer into the tokkuri as it warms (although there's no reason why you can't; see below for recommended temperatures). Real experts identify different stages in the training of a saké warmer, from pouring a little saké over the index finger, to watching how the saké at the top of the tokkuri gradually rises and becomes convex as it warms and expands, to the most delicate of all—instinct.

Whatever method you use, the important thing is to begin checking the warmth of the tokkuri almost as soon as you have put it in the warming pan. You can always put it back in, but once overheated, the saké is spoiled.

Traditional saké warmer for home use: a saucepan of water.

The debate over the proper temperature for serving saké warm dates back to the Edo period. The traditional formula is "another person's skin" (*hitohada*), but this only gives rise to more argument (suggested ways of judging "another person's skin" range from the highly practical to inserting your hand between your lover's thighs). Today, there are three ways to order saké warm in polite company, all variations on *kan o tsukete kudasai* ("please warm it"):

(1) *Nurukan* (lukewarm) is anywhere from room temperature to 40°C (104°F) and comes closest to the Edo-period ideal. If you drink slowly, you may find *nurukan* disagreeable, because the saké quickly cools. However, *nurukan* does not significantly alter the taste of the saké, and it is preferable to making saké hot and then letting it cool.

(2) *Kan* (warm), between 40° and 55°C (104° and 131°F), is the standard way of ordering saké today. The tokkuri should feel warm, but not quite hot. Most sakés served at this temperature will taste good even after they have cooled.

(3) *Atsukan* (hot), within the range of 55° to 60°C (131° to 140°F), causes problems, especially

Saké warmer for taking along to picnics and cherry-blossom viewings.

in the United States, where Japanese restaurants are used to catering to their customers' mistaken demands for piping hot saké. The tokkuri should feel hot, but not too hot to hold. If it is any hotter than this, you are well within your rights to send it back.

**Sharing** Whether the saké is warm or cold, drinking with tokkuri and sakazuki is one of the most enjoyable aspects of saké culture, for it is symbolic of a basic Japanese attitude toward drinking—that it is an act of communication and sharing. Small sakazuki empty quickly and need frequent refilling. In Japan, it is customary to perform *o-shaku*, that is, to pour for your drinking companion and to be poured for in return. This tiny ritual, repeated countless times over the course of an evening, can be a reaffirmation of an old friendship or the beginning of a new one, but it always implies a relationship, at least for that moment. The basic techniques of giving and receiving *o-shaku* may take some getting used to, but they are really quite sim-

Outdoor saké warmer. The cylinder at right holds the saké. In the bottom of the left cylinder is burning brushwood. The saké is warmed as it passes through the left cylinder to emerge from the spout.

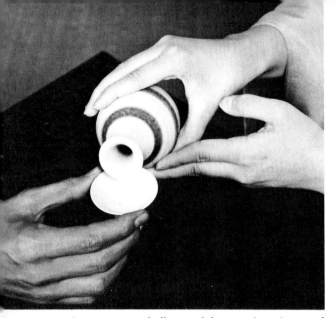

The proper way of offering *o-shaku*. Note how the tips of the fingers of the left hand support the tokkuri.

ple. They may also be applied when drinking beer, which is usually served in Japan in large 633-milliliter bottles with cups the size of juice glasses.

When receiving *o-shaku*, pick up the sakazuki with the thumb and index finger of your right hand, keeping them straight out and parallel to your chest. The other fingers should either be together and in line with your index finger (for larger sakazuki) or curled slightly toward your palm (for smaller sakazuki). When the pourer raises the tokkuri, extend the sakazuki toward him. Extend your left hand palm upward, keeping your fingers straight until the tip of your middle finger lightly supports the sakazuki in your right hand. Both your elbows should now be slightly extended but relaxed. Keep your eyes on your sakazuki. When it is nearly full, or if you do not want more to drink, raise it slightly, pushing up toward the inclined neck of the tokkuri. Raising the sakazuki before it is full is an important signal, indicating that you would like to drink more slowly for a few rounds. You may refuse an offer of saké politely by holding your hand palm down over your sakazuki, but it is more polite to accept a little saké at a time and make a pretense of drinking.

After receiving the saké you can either drink it at once or place the filled sakazuki on the table in front of you and immediately pour for your companion. Take the tokkuri in your right hand, holding it as you would a large sakazuki. As you extend the tokkuri, use your left hand palm upward in the same way you did when receiving,

lightly supporting the tokkuri with your fingertips. Swivel your wrist and tilt the tokkuri forward so that your palm is down as the saké pours out (this is important; pouring with your palm upward is likely to raise some eyebrows, for this is how bar hostesses and other women of the demimonde traditionally serve their customers).

*O-shaku* is a good example of the degrees of formality and the role of the sexes in the etiquette of drinking. In general these must be observed more strictly by women than by men. The techniques outlined above, for example, are always de rigueur for women, while a man who extends his left hand to support the sakazuki or tokkuri in anything but the most formal situations tends to look a bit affected. A man can usually give and accept *o-shaku* quite casually. Toward the end of an evening and in the company of intimates, it is quite acceptable to pour for yourself, although it is customary to offer saké first to the others at your table. Pouring for yourself, in fact, is perversely a sign of great friendship.

## Other Ways of Drinking

Another interesting way to drink saké is from the small wooden boxes called *masu*. Casks and bottles of saké are still made according to traditional Japanese volume measures. A masu holds 0.18 liter of saké, called 1 *gō*, meaning that there are exactly

Typical shapes of sakazuki.

Masu and a small cask for holding the saké and giving it a woody flavor.

Besides the three- to five-tiered sets of sakazuki used in Shinto rituals, tokkuri with sakazuki, and masu, there are many other kinds of utensils used for drinking saké. The practice of using teacups for saké evolved into a new type of fine pottery called *guinomi* (literally, "chugging cups"). These cups are designed for the solitary drinker who doesn't want to bother with tokkuri and sakazuki and just wants to get on with the drinking.

One of the most interesting ways to drink saké is called *hire-zake*. *Hire* is the dried fin of the famous delicacy *fugu*, a kind of blowfish or globefish whose meat is used in soups after the poisonous bladder has been removed by a specially trained chef. The fins, you will be pleased to know, are non-toxic. A small piece of *hire* is put into a cup, usually a beer glass, of saké, and the saké is then warmed. The fin gives the saké a mellow, smoky flavor highly prized by connoisseurs. Today, *hire-zake* is available in many drinking places in Japan.

ten of them in the standard *isshō-bin* ("1-*shō* bottle") of 1.8 liters. Originally masu were the smallest of the wooden boxes used as rice measures. Cheap and readily available, they were ideal for serving saké at festivals and other large gatherings. In the drinking places of the Edo and Meiji periods, they also served to measure out the saké and demonstrate to the customer that he was getting his money's worth.

This function of masu is reflected in the etiquette of serving them today. The empty masu is placed before the customer on a small saucer and then filled from a larger vessel until a little saké spills over the sides, demonstrating that a full measure has been served. The custom of serving a small dish of salt with the masu also dates back to the old *izakaya*, where salt was often the only sakana served with saké. Drinking from a masu is simple. Just choose a corner and sip, holding one side with your right hand, thumb on the top and the other fingers on the bottom, and supporting the other side lightly with your left hand. The salt may be sprinkled on the rim at this corner (not too much, or you'll ruin the saké) just before you sip, or you can make a fist with your free hand and sprinkle salt in the depression formed by your thumb and index finger, tequila style. Saké in masu is never warmed.

Masu are also often used at receptions, outdoor parties, festivals, and other large celebrations where a *komodaru*, or wooden party cask, is to be opened. In restaurants and drinking places, saké casks are usually tapped from the bottom, like wine or whiskey barrels, but at parties the cask will be cracked open from the top with a mallet, and the saké served with a new bamboo ladle. At a Japanese-style wedding reception, for example, the bride and bridegroom will break open the top together, in a ritual that is the Japanese equivalent of cutting the first slice of a wedding cake.

## Purchase and Storage

While a few outstanding *ginjō* sakés may age well, most sakés are best when drunk young. When buying sakés, always check the date on the label. Do not buy a saké that has been in the bottle much over one year, and drink older sakés fairly soon after purchase. Before it is opened, saké can be stored in any cool, dry place out of direct sunlight. Wrapping the bottle in opaque paper can be useful. Saké deteriorates rapidly after opening as a result of oxidation, and can become quite bitter. You should consider this when deciding what size bottle to buy. The standard 1.8-liter bottle is ideal for parties, but not very practical for drink-

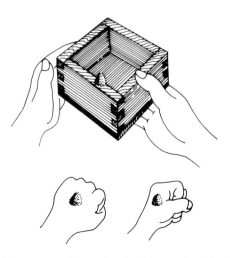

Holding a masu. Salt can be placed just to the side of a corner or on the fist.

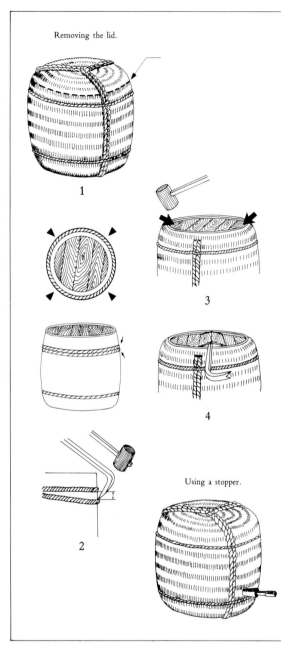

Removing the lid.

1

2

3

4

Using a stopper.

## HOW TO OPEN A PARTY CASK (*KOMODARU*)

*1. Using a pair of scissors along the top edge of the cask, cut the reed-mat wrapping. Cut the outer ropes that hold the wrapping in place and slip the cask out. Brush off any shreds of the mat from the top of the cask.*

*2. Two ropes bind the cask at the very top. Lowering these will relieve the pressure on the lid and make it easier to remove. Insert a crowbar between the ropes and, at four places equally spaced around the circumference of the cask, pound gently with a mallet until the lower rope slips about a finger's width down the side. Now repeat for the upper rope, lowering it until the two ropes are together again. Do not cut the ropes or remove them.*

*3. With a hammer, strike the shortest slats of the lid at an angle so that, as they push toward the center, the lid bends up slightly in the middle.*

*4. Pry up the center slats of the lid with the pointed end of the crowbar until you can remove them with your hands.*

*After you have removed all the slats of the lid, ladle out any scraps of matting floating in the saké (or use a tea strainer). For traditional-style Japanese ceremonies, the slats are now put back in place on top of the lid. Then, at a wedding party, for example, the bride and groom "open" the prepared cask with a light strike of the mallet. The saké is ladled out to the guests, who receive it in wooden masu for toasting the newlyweds. If you simply want to drink the saké, which will have a luscious, woody flavor, you can dispense with the ceremony and use your masu as a scoop to dip in to your heart's content. You can also serve from the cask beer-barrel style. There should be a plug near the base of the cask, which you can pry out and replace with a wedge-shaped stopper instead of banging open the slats at the top. (Before removing the plug, place the cask on its side with the plug at the top; if you don't, saké will pour out before you have a chance to insert the stopper.) Once the cask is opened, the saké should be drunk within two weeks. Since a party cask will hold 18 or 36 liters (larger sizes are also available) make sure you have plenty of friends around to help complete the job.*

ing alone or in small groups. Refrigeration helps, but only for a while. Generally speaking, a saké that has been open over a month is best used as a cooking wine. When the saké becomes cloudy, or develops a distinct vinegary smell, throw it away.

## Banqueting, with Saké

Occasions for banquets, both formal and informal, are numerous in Japan, and today many Japanese restaurants in the United States have tatami banquet rooms (*zashiki*). The formal banquet in Japan is often compared to the tea ceremony, and complete mastery of all the etiquette of dining on tatami is an elusive goal even for the connoisseur. Most Japanese hold banquets for much the same reasons that Americans do—to celebrate special occasions, to establish or cement relationships, or to conduct business—and the trend is toward less formality. If you attend a banquet, you needn't worry too much about decorum. Your status as a foreigner guarantees that you will be forgiven even the most serious gaffes. But the more you know of the basic rules of the game, the more impressive you will be to your hosts, who may unabashedly cluck with delight over your every correct move. The following pointers will get you through even the most formal banquet, and many of them will be useful in any drinking situation.

PRELIMINARIES

Basic preparations for any banquet include a good supply of business or name cards, a handkerchief, and clean socks or stockings (because you always take your shoes off before stepping into a tatami room). Your shoes should be polished and relatively new, and easy to get in and out of. The average banquet lasts at least two hours, and since you will be sitting on the tatami and shifting your legs about, be sure to wear loose-fitting trousers, or pleated or flared skirts of modest length.

The typical banquet room is rectangular and has a ceremonial alcove (the *tokonoma*) in one wall, usually opposite the entrance. The seat nearest this alcove, or furthest from the entrance, is the *kamiza* (''highest seat''), and the seat nearest the entrance is the *shimoza* (''lowest seat''). The host will take the lowest seat after everyone else has been seated. The highest seat is reserved for the guest of honor, and everyone else will take places roughly according to their age and status in the group. People of lower status usually arrive early and wait for higher-ranking guests and the guest of honor.

A banquet room at the beautifully styled Oimatsu restaurant in Fukuoka City. The figure at right shows the seats of the guest of honor and the host.

Therefore, it is extremely important to be on time.

When you enter the banquet room, quietly find a place to sit. Greetings and introductions will take place later. If you are the guest of honor, or one of the important guests, your host will ask you to sit at the highest seat or indicate a place close to it. Otherwise, try to find a place near the lowest seat, or better yet, find a seat near someone you know. Most banquet rooms have low tables with cushions for sitting (*zabuton*) arranged around them on the tatami. At formal banquets, there may be small tables (*zen*) for each person.

There are both formal and informal ways of sit-

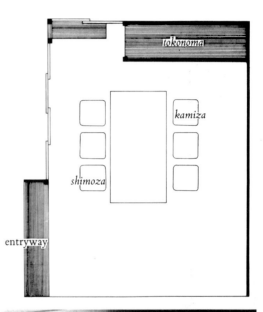

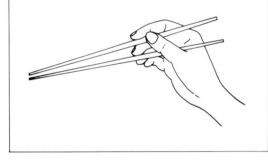
ting on *zabuton*. The formal sitting posture is called *seiza*, and is correct for both men and women at the beginning of a banquet. Kneel directly in the center of the *zabuton* and then, keeping your back straight, lower your hips so that they are resting on your heels. Extend your feet backward and cross them, the instep of your right foot in the arch of your left. Your knees should be in line with the edge of the table.

Few people can maintain this posture for the duration of a banquet. After about five or ten minutes the pain becomes excrutiating, accompanied by involuntary twitching and an inability to pay attention to the obligatory speeches or, worse, the food. At informal banquets more comfortable positions are assumed almost from the beginning. Men can cross their legs in front of them Indian style. The

informal posture for women is only a slight improvement on *seiza* in terms of comfort. The best way to achieve it is to imagine your hips falling off your heels to the right, with a slight shifting of your legs to the left. You will still be sitting with your back straight and your legs tucked up beside you, but at least you will no longer be sitting on them, and they should not fall asleep in this position.

MANNERS

The banquet will begin with greetings from the host and a toast (*kampai*). When seated at larger tables, people exchange *o-shaku* with those on either side of them. The opening toast is the occasion for the most formal *o-shaku* etiquette. Saké will be served throughout the meal, and the exchange of *o-shaku* will gradually become more relaxed. Watch the other guests and follow their lead. Don't persist in formal gestures after everyone else has begun to relax.

A few of the details of handling eating utensils may take some getting used to. A pair of chopsticks will be at your place at the table lying across a small bridge-shaped chopstick stand. When you reach for them, your fingers should be in the same position as for picking up a sakazuki, but pointing down. Transfer them to your left hand and align the two tips with your right. Then grasp them again with your right hand, in a comfortable position for manipulation. By now most Westerners are familiar with how to use chopsticks for picking up small bits of food from a plate. When eating rice, however, you should cup the rice bowl in your hand, lift it up toward you, and "shovel" the rice into your mouth.

Soups are often served in bowls with tight-fitting covers. Remove the cover as soon as the soup is placed before you. Steady the bowl with your left hand, remove the cover with your right, and set the cover upside down on the table. Pick the bowl up with your right hand and then transfer it to your left (thumb on the rim, fingertips supporting the base). Bring the bowl up to your mouth, tilt it, and sip (it is acceptable to slurp). Use your chopsticks to pick out fish and vegetables. Be sure to put the cover back on the bowl (not upside down) when you have finished the soup.

One final note. Before you at any one time there may be half a dozen or more different dishes. It is considered polite to sample them in the order they were served, but not to finish an entire dish all at once. Pick a little from each in turn.

# Food with Saké: Sakana

Over the course of a traditional Japanese banquet, or at a drinking establishment, you will partake of as many as a dozen small dishes: slices of raw fish, grilled meats, stews and broths, legumes, vegetables, fish cakes, tofu. All of these foods are sakana—the cuisine of saké—the principle being that saké does not accompany the food but food complements the saké. These dishes resemble nothing more than a procession of hors d'oeuvres, and indeed, to the Japanese, the real "meal" is the rice served at the end, usually with miso soup, pickled vegetables, and green tea, after the saké drinking is over. Saké is liquid rice, and because saké and rice are so closely related they do not appear on the table together.

The close connection between food and saké means that the true saké connoisseur is a gourmet as well as a discriminating drinker. The lover of good food in Japan values subtle, natural flavors over heavy sauces, and prides himself on knowing exactly what to order in each season and how to orchestrate the sequence of dishes. This is no small accomplishment, for the variety of seafood, vegetables, plants, and other ingredients used in Japanese cuisine goes far beyond anything imaginable in the West, and there is a wide range of local and regional cuisines to choose from. The gourmet tastes with his eye as well as his palate, and he looks not only at the arrangement of food on each individual dish,

but also at the shapes of the dishes and the skill with which the chef has coordinated their colors and textures to add grace, rhythm, and body to the meal. While superficially the impact of Japanese food on the palate is understated, to the connoisseur a proper service is a splendid symphony of complex subtleties and seasonal nuances. Your tray in early spring may contain a tiny arrangement of fresh green mountain vegetables garnished with a sprig of pink cherry blossoms collected that very morning at a site miles away from the restaurant. The saké chosen to accompany this scene must wash it gently and soothe it to perfection.

The menus presented on the following two pages, one for spring–summer and another for autumn–winter, reflect these aspects of Japanese cuisine, as well as the typical sequence of serving sakana at a banquet or ordering in a restaurant. The purist would demand a menu for each season, and the connoisseur might insist that further distinctions be made for all of the subtle shifts that occur within seasons. Most restaurants and drinking places, however, have printed menus similar to these, with perennial favorites available all year round. Seasonal dishes, or recommended dishes, are usually handwritten on a separate menu. At a banquet, of course, everything is done for you, and some restaurants have suggested courses for people who do not want to be bothered with ordering each dish individually. Often, however, you will be on your own. Especially in drinking establishments you can order several times during the evening, selecting dishes pretty much as the fancy strikes you.

Spring–summer.

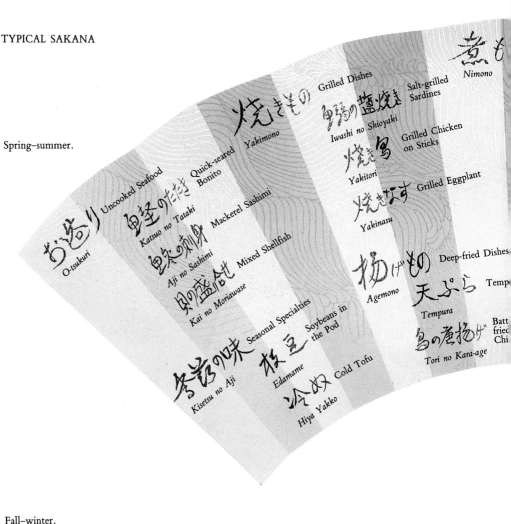

お造り O-tsukuri Uncooked Seafood

鰹のたたき Katsuo no Tataki Quick-seared Bonito

鯵の刺身 Aji no Sashimi Mackerel Sashimi

貝の盛合せ Kai no Moriawase Mixed Shellfish

季節の味 Kisetsu no Aji Seasonal Specialties

枝豆 Edamame Soybeans in the Pod

冷奴 Hiya Yakko Cold Tofu

焼きもの Yakimono Grilled Dishes

鰯の塩焼き Iwashi no Shioyaki Salt-grilled Sardines

焼き鳥 Yakitori Grilled Chicken on Sticks

焼きなす Yakinasu Grilled Eggplant

揚げもの Agemono Deep-fried Dishes

天ぷら Tempura Tempura

鳥の唐揚げ Tori no Kara-age Batter-fried Chicken

煮もの Nimono Nimono

Fall–winter.

鍋もの Nabemono One-pot Dishes

湯豆腐 Yudōfu Simmering Tofu

よせ鍋 Yosenabe Fish and Vegetable Hot-Pot

鳥の水たき Tori no Mizutaki Chicken Hot-Pot

おでん Oden Vegetable and Fishcake Stew

お造り O-tsukuri Uncooked Seafood

鮪の刺身 Maguro no Sashimi Tuna Sashimi

いかの刺身 Ika no Sashimi Squid Sashimi

はまちの刺身 Hamachi no Sashimi Yellowtail Sashimi

煮もの Nimono Simmered Dishes

ぶり大根 Buri Daikon Simmered Yellowtail with Radish

肉じゃが Nikujaga Potato Stew with Pork

煮こみ Nikomi Chicken Innards in Miso Broth

切干大根 Kiriboshi Daikon Stewed Radish Strips

あさりの酒蒸し Asari no Sakamushi Steamed Clams

揚げもの Agemono Deep-fried Dishes

あげだし豆腐 Agedashi-dōfu Deep-fried Tofu

かれいの唐揚げ Karei no Kara-age Batter-fried Sole

mmered Dishes

あえもの Aemono "Dressed" Dishes

ん煮 Wakatake-ni — Bamboo Shoots and Wakame Seaweed

いんげんのごまあえ Ingen no Goma-ae — Green Beans with Sesame Dressing

ひらごぼう Kimpira Gobō — Piquant Simmered Burdock

じき Hijiki — Hijiki Seaweed

和風サラダ Wafū Sarada — Salad with Soy Sauce and Sesame Dressing

もろきゅう Morokyū — Cucumbers with Miso Dip

るもの Sunomono — Vinegared Dishes

きゅうり酢 Kyūri-zu — Vinegared Cucumbers

ひもの Himono — Dried Foods

魚のぬた Maguro no Nuta — Tuna with Light Miso Dressing

めざし Mezashi — Dried Sardines

するめ Surume — Dried Squid

おしんこ O-shinko — Pickled Dishes

きゅうりの糠漬け Kyūri no Nukazuke — Cucumbers Pickled in Rice Bran

かぶの浅漬け Kabu no Asazuke — Fast Turnip Pickles

らっきょう Rakkyō — Shallots

焼もの Yakimono — Grilled Dishes

さんまの塩焼き Samma no Shioyaki — Salt-grilled **Saury**

ぶりの照り焼き Buri no Teriyaki — Yellowtail Teriyaki

なすの田楽 Nasu no Dengaku — Eggplant with Sweet Miso Sauce

酢のもの Sunomono — Vinegared Dishes

わかめ酢 Wakame-zu — Vinegared Wakame Seaweed

といいも酢のもの Yamaimo no Sunomono — Mountain Yams

あえもの Aemono — "Dressed" Dishes

ほうれん草のおひたし Hōrensō no O-hitashi — Spinach Garnished with Bonito Shavings

なめこおろし Nameko Oroshi — Mushrooms and Grated White Radish

珍味 Chimmi — Rare Delicacies

塩から Shiokara — Fresh Salted Squid

あん肝 Ankimo — Livers of Anglerfish

99

Spring. Bamboo shoots are a springtime treat, and the presence of various foods on skewers suggests the practice of eating outdoors while enjoying the flowers and warm weather in early April. A cherry blossom garnishes the plate at upper right.

Summer. Trout and conger eel are seasonal specialities, as is the *sushi* wrapped in bamboo grass at right. Serving boxes with open slats suggest cooling breezes.

## The Menus

Japanese menus are usually arranged in the following order, which with a few additions is also the authentic course of a full banquet: fresh, uncooked fish (*o-tsukuri*); grilled dishes (*yakimono*); simmered dishes (*nimono*); deep-fried dishes (*agemono*); vinegared dishes (*sunomono*); "dressed" dishes (*aemono*); "rare delicacies" (*chimmi*); and rice dishes (*shokuji*, usually not served with saké). In late autumn and winter, one-pot dishes (*nabemono*) may replace grilled, simmered, and deep-fried foods on the seasonal menu. Specialty restaurants, such as *sushi* bars, will not have the full range of dishes. At an *izakaya*, where the main objective is to drink saké, one seldom orders from every category on the menu, and servings tend to be smaller.

The basic sequence of a full meal is light—heavy—light—rice, reflecting the division of the meal into three distinct parts. The meal begins with *o-tsukuri*, which is usually served by itself or with a clear soup. The heartier grilled, simmered, and deep-fried dishes are served in the middle, while such light, highly flavored dishes as vinegared dishes, "dressed" foods, and delicacies are eaten toward the end to refresh the palate. Sakés usually follow the same general pattern, with the added dimension of dry—sweet—dry—stop. When you are drinking, however, a series of very light dishes is often preferable, especially if there is a selection of really outstanding sakés. The recipes that follow this section on pages 102–9 will give you a good idea of the range of simple sakanas and more hearty dishes. Try several of them some evening, with saké, as an alternative to the conventional Western-style dinner; you will get full, but at a comfortable pace and in an atmosphere of genial conversation.

The seasonal aspect of Japanese cuisine is reflected in both the ingredients of dishes and the way they are prepared. Modern techniques in agriculture and fishing have made most ingredients available all year round, but traditional associations still play an important role. Tuna (*maguro*) is best in winter, when it is heavy with fat, while young bamboo shoots (*wakatake*) are firmly associated with spring. Many of the seasonal principles of preparation will be familiar to anyone—cold tofu (*hiya yakko*) in summer, simmering tofu (*yudōfu*) in autumn and winter, for example.

Similarly, lighter foods are preferred in the spring and summer, while heavier dishes are ideal in colder seasons.

The category of *o-tsukuri* represents the ultimate in Japanese cuisine. These dishes should always be ordered first, so that the delicate flavors of the uncooked seafood can be appreciated before the palate is sated. This is also the time to order the best saké in the house, preferably one that is light and relatively dry. A fine *ginjō* saké is ideal, and you will want to order it *hiya* (room temperature) or slightly chilled.

*Sashimi*, slices of raw fish or shellfish, is usually served with a dipping sauce of soy sauce and green horseradish (*wasabi*). The dipping sauce for *tataki*

Autumn. A banquet of seasonal allusions. *Sushi* on the platter at upper right has been sculpted into the shapes of chrysanthemum flowers. The *tempura* at upper left has been arranged to look like a basket of fallen leaves. Mushrooms, chestnuts, and mackerel are all foods that are best in the autumn.

Winter. The custom is to enjoy saké while admiring a fresh snowfall. Hot, simmering tofu is in the container at upper left, and at lower right is another seasonal clue: salmon eggs packed into a fresh citron. A variety of deep-fried foods make this a hearty meal on a cold day.

is soy sauce with grated ginger and chopped green onions. Both of these sauces are best suited to a dry saké. But *usu-zukuri* dishes, in which the fish is cut into paper-thin slices, are served with a sauce called *ponzu*, basically a combination of soy sauce, vinegar, and citrus juice. The high acidity of this sauce will soften a sweet saké and bring out its other flavors. But you will want to avoid *usu-zukuri* when drinking full-bodied sakés, whether dry or sweet, because the high acidity of the saké will clash with the acids of the *ponzu*.

*Ponzu* is also the basic dressing for vinegared foods and is used as a dipping sauce for many one-pot dishes, such as the familiar *shabu shabu* using paper-thin strips of raw beef, and some of the grilled and deep-fried foods. While these dishes may complement sweeter sakés, avoid them if the saké you are drinking has a high acidity.

Things become somewhat more complicated in the other categories. In general, the pattern of full-bodied sakés with heavier dishes and stronger tastes holds, but sweetness is also an important factor. For example, *yakitori* (grilled chicken on sticks) is good with any light saké when it is salt-grilled, but *yakitori* grilled with the sweet sauce called *tare* almost demands a dry, full-bodied saké.

Similarly, salt-grilled fish goes better with light sakés, while *teriyaki* complements sakés that have more body.

There is also a wide range of dishes in the category of simmered dishes (*nimono*). Young bamboo shoots are simmered in an extremely light sauce with just a dash of soy sauce and a little saké. A full-bodied saké would overpower this dish. Heartier dishes, such as potato stew with pork (*nikujaga*) or yellowtail with white radish (*buri daikon*), are excellent with full-bodied sakés. These dishes tend to be sweet, so you will also want to select relatively dry sakés.

There are two basic types of dishes in the category of deep-fried foods: *tempura* and thick-battered "Chinese-fried" (*kara-age*). The lighter *tempura* is accompanied by light sakés, with many people preferring them to be on the sweet side. The Chinese-fried dishes are more problematic. In general they demand more full-bodied sakés. This is certainly true of chicken and fish with stronger flavors, but a light, delicate fish such as sole (*karei*) may taste better with a lighter saké. Again, you will want to avoid heavier sakés if a *ponzu* dipping sauce is served.

Vinegared dishes (*sunomono*), dried foods (*himono*), and the "rare delicacies" (*chimmi*) follow *o-tsukuri* in the hierarchy of sakana, and *chimmi* dishes spring to mind first when one thinks about sakana for drinking. If you have switched to a lesser saké during the middle of a meal, this is the time to go back to top-grade sakés. Some of these dishes may sound (and look) a little intimidating—livers of anglerfish (*ankimo*), and eel pickled with salt and its own intestines, for instance. But they are well worth trying, because their distinctive flavors make them ideally suited to the very best sakés, especially light *ginjō* types.

Rice-Cracker Canapés.

Mushroom Sauté.

Won-ton Twist Fries.

Hard-boiled Egg Halves.

Radish and Salmon Rolls.

Eggplant with Miso Sauce.

Grilled Ginger Beef.

Crab and Kiwi Salad.

Grilled Chicken on Sticks (*Yakitori*)
with Skins in Sweet Sauce.

Scallops and Watercress.

## Sakana for Your Table (1)

Here are some simple dishes perfect for an evening at home drinking saké and relaxing. Mix and match to suit your taste. All the ingredients you need for these recipes, and the ones on pages 108–9, are available at regular supermarkets or Oriental groceries (where you can ask for the item by its Japanese name; in some cases, substitutes are suggested). ABBREVIATIONS: Tbsp = tablespoon, tsp = teaspoon, g = gram, cm = centimeter, oz = ounce, lb = pound, '' = inch. Metric and American equivalents are approximate.

### Rice-Cracker Canapés          (serves 2)

**6 thin, lightly salted rice crackers (usuyaki sembei) or any lightly salted crackers**

SPREAD A
**1 Tbsp bottled sea urchin paste (neriuni)**
**1 hard-boiled egg yolk**
**1/5 tsp soy sauce**

SPREAD B
**2 Tbsp cottage cheese**
**1 Tbsp mayonnaise**

CAVIAR-RADISH TOPPING
**2 thin rounds of giant white radish (daikon)**
**1 tsp caviar**

Make spreads A and B. Spread or spoon onto crackers. Lay 1 slice radish on each of remaining crackers and top with 1/2 tsp caviar. Arrange and serve.

### Radish and Salmon Rolls          (serves 2)

**5-cm (2'') length giant white radish (daikon)**
**6 slices smoked salmon, each about 8 cm (3'') long**
**2 green onion tops or young scallions (Japanese asatsuki, if available)**
**6 capers**

Peel white radish and cut into rectangular strips, each 1/2 × 1/2 × 5 cm (1/8 × 1/8 × 2''). Cut onions into 5-cm (2'') lengths. Roll 4 to 5 strips radish and 2 pieces onion in 1 slice salmon. Place seam side face down on serving plate, top with capers, and serve.

### Won-ton Twist Fries          (serves 2)

**6 won-ton skins**
**vegetable oil for deep-frying**
**salt**
**ketchup**

FILLING
**1 Tbsp finely chopped salami**
**1 Tbsp grated cheddar cheese**
**1 Tbsp finely chopped onion**

Mix filling ingredients. Divide filling into 6 portions. Place 1 portion filling in center of each skin, bring up corners, and twist to seal. Heat oil to 160°C (320°F) for deep-frying. Fry until skin is golden brown, turning occasionally. Serve hot. Sprinkle with salt or dip in ketchup.

### Mushroom Sauté          (serves 2)

**4 fresh Chinese black mushrooms (shiitake)**
**115 g (4 oz) shimeji mushrooms**
**40 g (1 1/2 oz) enokidake mushrooms**
**[mushrooms listed above can be replaced by any available American varieties]**
**2 Tbsp butter**
**salt**
**pepper**
**1 tsp soy sauce**

Wash mushrooms well and pat dry. Remove stems from Chinese black mushrooms. Trim stems of remaining mushrooms. Sauté whole mushrooms in butter (start with Chinese mushrooms, then add smaller shimeji and enokidake). Season with salt and pepper to taste. When mushrooms are done, add soy sauce and sauté mushrooms a few seconds longer. Serve immediately.

### Hard-boiled Egg Halves          (serves 2)

**2 hard-boiled eggs**
**1/2 cup soy sauce**
**1/2 cup saké**

Peel hard-boiled eggs. In a small pot simmer egg with soy sauce and saké for 20 minutes, turning egg occasionally to ensure even coloring and cooking. Cut each egg in half lengthwise and serve.

## Eggplant with Miso Sauce    (serves 2)

140 g (5 oz) eggplant, about 1/2 medium
    eggplant
oil for sautéing
1/2 tsp toasted sesame seeds

MISO SAUCE
1 Tbsp red miso
1 Tbsp sugar
1 Tbsp saké
1 Tbsp mirin (sweet cooking saké)

Mix ingredients for miso sauce and place in
double boiler, stirring constantly until thick
and smooth (5–8 minutes). Cut eggplant into 1-cm (1/2'') rounds and sauté in oil. Drain
on absorbent paper. Spread on miso sauce, top
with toasted sesame seeds, and serve.

## Crab and Kiwi Salad    (serves 2)

1 kiwifruit
115 g (4 oz) crab meat, canned, boiled,
    or steamed

DRESSING
1 Tbsp rice vinegar
1 tsp sugar
1/2 tsp soy sauce

Peel kiwifruit and cut into 1/2-cm (1/8'')
rounds. Line inside of small bowl with
kiwifruit rounds. Drain crab, remove any car-
tilage and shell, break meat into chunks, and
place in bowl. Combine ingredients for dressing and pour over crab and kiwifruit just
before serving.

## Scallops and Watercress    (serves 2)

6 watercress tops
115 g (4 oz) scallops, boiled

DRESSING
1 Tbsp miso
1 Tbsp rice vinegar
1/2 Tbsp saké
1/2 Tbsp mirin (sweet cooking saké)

Wash watercress and tear roughly into thirds.
Break scallop meat into chunks. Cream miso
with vinegar, saké, and mirin until smooth.
Mix scallops and watercress together in bowl
and top with dressing.

## Grilled Ginger Beef    (serves 2)

200 g (7 oz) choice beef, rump, or
    tenderloin
1 green onion, finely chopped
1/2 clove garlic, finely chopped
1 tsp finely grated fresh ginger
2 tsp soy sauce

Broil meat (or pan-fry with oil) on both sides
until surface is a light brown. Cool beef and
slice into bite-size chunks. Top beef with
onion, ginger, and garlic. Season each serving with 1 tsp soy sauce.

## Grilled Chicken on Sticks (*Yakitori*) with Skins in Sweet Sauce    (serves 2)

1 large chicken thigh, with skin
15-cm (6'') bamboo skewers or sharp
    metal skewers

YAKITORI
4 Tbsp soy sauce
2 Tbsp mirin (sweet cooking saké)
*shichimi tōgarashi* (a mixture of red
    pepper flakes, ground orange peel, and
    other spices) or ground red pepper

SWEET SAUCE
1 Tbsp soy sauce
3 Tbsp saké
1 tsp slivered ginger

YAKITORI
Immerse bamboo skewers in water for several
minutes. Combine soy sauce and mirin in
saucepan and place over medium heat until
liquid is reduced by about half. Remove skin
from chicken. Reserve skin and cut meat into 2 1/2-cm (1'') cubes. Thread 3 or 4 chunks
of meat on each skewer. Barbecue or broil
skewers until lightly browned on one side;
brush with sauce. Broil again on other side;
brush with sauce. Repeat until meat is done.
Serve at once. Brush with more sauce or
season sparingly with *shichimi tōgarashi* or red
pepper to taste.

SKINS
Place skin from chicken in water and bring
to a boil. Remove skin and wash thoroughly
in cold water to remove oil. Boil in fresh
water and wash again. Cut skin into 1/2-cm
(1/8'') strips and simmer with soy sauce, saké,
and ginger for 3–4 minutes. Serve.

Winter Hot-Pot.

Chicken Hot-Pot.

Simmering Tofu.

## Sakana for Your Table (2)

These dishes can be made right at the table in front of your guests, who choose items from the pot as they please. The two hot-pots make nutritious filling meals in wintertime.

| Winter Hot-Pot | (serves 4) |
|---|---|

**250 g (9 oz) white fish, filleted**

**280 g (10 oz) raw oysters**

**8 fresh clams**

**4 jumbo shrimp**

**1 block tofu, about 280 g (10 oz)**

**8 fresh Chinese black mushrooms (*shiitake*) or white mushrooms**

**200 g (7 oz) *shirataki* (*sukiyaki* noodles: gelatinous filaments made from devil's tongue plant)**

**13 cm (5") carrot**

**2–3 leaves Chinese cabbage**

**115 g (4 oz) chrysanthemum leaves (*shungiku*) or spinach**

**2 leeks**

CHICKEN

**280 g (10 oz) ground chicken**

**3 Tbsp grated onion**

**1 egg**

**1 1/2 Tbsp cornstarch**

**1 tsp saké**

**1/5 tsp salt**

BROTH

**5 cups *dashi* (bonito fish stock; you can use the powdered, instant variety)**

**3 Tbsp saké**

**2 Tbsp soy sauce**

**1 Tbsp mirin**

**1 tsp salt**

CONDIMENTS

**2 green onions, thinly sliced**

**juice from 1 lemon**

***shichimi tōgarashi* (a mixture of red pepper flakes, ground orange peel, and other spices) or ground pepper**

PREPARATION

1. To remove sand and grit, soak clams in salt water until ready to use. Rinse oysters in salt water several times, then drain in colander.
2. Shell and de-vein shrimp, but leave tail and last section of shell in place.
3. Cut tofu into 2 1/2-cm (1") cubes. Drain in colander.
4. Remove stems from mushrooms.
5. Parboil *shirataki* for 2–3 minutes. Drain.
6. Cut carrot crosswise into 1/2-cm (1/8") pieces.
7. Cut Chinese cabbage leaves into 5-cm (2") squares.
8. Cut chrysanthemum leaves or spinach into 5-cm (2") lengths.
9. Slice leeks diagonally at 1-cm (1/2") intervals.

CHICKEN

10. Mix ingredients for meatballs thoroughly until they form a thick paste.
11. Roll mixture between palms to form golfball-size meatballs.
12. Boil meatballs in water for 3–5 minutes.

COOKING AND SERVING

13. Put some of each ingredient in an attractive pot or casserole.
14. Arrange the remaining ingredients on a separate dish.
15. Using another pot, combine ingredients for broth and bring to a boil.
16. Pour broth into pot with ingredients. Place this pot on a heating element or hot plate and simmer at the table until ingredients are ready (some will cook more quickly than others).
17. Diners pick from pot as they choose. Dip simmered foods in lemon juice if desired (or use *ponzu* sauce as in Chicken Hot-Pot) and use condiments to taste.
18. Add more ingredients and hot broth as needed.

## Simmering Tofu (serves 2)

1 block tofu, about 280 g (10 oz)
8 × 18-cm (3 × 7") piece dried kelp
  (*kombu*)
2 medium-size dried Chinese black
  mushrooms (*shiitake*)

CONDIMENTS
2 green onions, finely chopped
2 chopped green *shiso* (beefsteak plant)
  leaves
1/4 cup lightly packed dried bonito
  shavings
2 Tbsp finely grated ginger
soy sauce

1. Soak dried mushrooms in 1/2 cup tepid water for 40 minutes. Remove stems and cut caps into thirds. Reserve soaking water to use as stock.
2. Wipe kelp with damp cloth. Cut kelp crosswise into 1-cm (1/2") wide strips and soak in 6 cups water for 30 minutes.
3. Cut tofu into 4 pieces.
4. Add mushrooms and reserved water to kelp stock. Add tofu to stock and heat over low flame.
5. When tofu rises to surface, remove it from pot with wire-mesh skimmer and place atop *shiso* leaves on individual plates. Top with condiments as desired and season with soy sauce to taste.

## Chicken Hot-Pot (serves 4)

450 g (1 lb) chicken, thigh or breast
10-cm (4") square dried kelp (*kombu*)
115 g (4 oz) chrysanthemum leaves
  (*shungiku*) or spinach
1 block wheat gluten (*fu*; available in
  dried form in Oriental groceries) or 1
  block tofu
8 fresh Chinese black mushrooms
  (*shiitake*)
1/2 cup saké

PONZU SAUCE
1/2 cup lemon juice
1/2 cup soy sauce
1/4 cup chicken stock (see step 2) or
  water

CONDIMENTS
1/2 cup giant white radish, grated and
  seasoned with ground red pepper
2 leeks, finely chopped, then soaked and
  drained
2 green onions, finely chopped

PREPARATION
1. Cut chicken into bite-size chunks. Pour boiling water over chicken placed in colander.
2. Wipe kelp with damp cloth. In a large pot, add kelp, chicken, and an ample amount of water. Bring to a boil over high heat and remove kelp just before water boils. Reduce heat to low, add saké, and simmer for 30 minutes, occasionally skimming off fat and foam.
3. Remove chicken from pot and strain broth.
4. Combine ingredients for *ponzu* sauce and prepare condiments.
5. Cut chrysanthemum leaves (or spinach) into 5-cm (2") lengths.
6. Soften dried wheat gluten in warm water for 5–10 minutes. Squeeze out excess water, then cut gluten (or tofu) into 2 1/2-cm (1") cubes.
7. Remove stems from mushrooms.

COOKING AND SERVING
8. Put chicken and broth back in pot and bring to a boil. Add some of each ingredient. Transfer pot to heating element or hot plate at the table.
9. Diners select cooked ingredients from pot and dip into sauce (add condiments to sauce as desired).
10. Add more ingredients and broth as needed.

Edo Masa: *noren* with design of cards presented by the sumo wrestler Washūyama. Ryōgoku, Tokyo.

Tarumatsu: serving *taru-zake*. Ueno, Tokyo.

Gombei: country-inn-style interior. Akita City.

Tako Ume: shopfront with lantern and *noren*. Nihombashi, Osaka.

Daikoku: *noren* with design of treasure mallet. Kuroe-monchō, Osaka.

Hisago: *noren* with design of gourds. Shinjuku, Tokyo.

Sasaya: shopfront with rope *noren*. Kyōbashi, Tokyo.

Dōraku: *noren* made of gourds. Honchō, Tokyo.

Kuremutsu: approach garden. Asakusa, Tokyo.

# Izakaya: Great Places to Drink Saké

Any dedicated saké lover will tell you that the ideal place to enjoy saké is an *izakaya*. Ask what an *izakaya* is, however, and you will receive a bewildering array of answers. Literally translated, the word *izakaya* means a "sit-down saké shop." *Izakaya* first appeared in the early Edo period, when saké dealers began supplementing their profits by setting up tables and benches in their shops and serving cheap saké by the masu. Their customers were itinerant laborers and other poor townsmen, unable to afford more elegant surroundings or anything more delectable than a little salt as a sakana. The idea was to get drunk as cheaply as possible. Similar drinking places still exist today, but the true *izakaya* has evolved into something quite different.

When the Japanese saké drinker waxes eloquent on the subject of *izakaya*, he first distinguishes them from *nomiya* (bars) and *taishū sakaba* (pubs), which are basically indiscriminate watering holes. This distinction is largely in the eye of the beholder. A great many places that call themselves *izakaya* would not fit the connoisseur's ideal image, while an equal number that are called something else would—a *yakitori* or *oden* shop, for example. The distinction mostly has to do with size, mood, and subtle differences in the behavior that is expected from customers.

Most large bars and pubs in Japan resemble their counterparts in the West; they are crowded, rowdy, and fun. Food is prepared in great quantities, and served with a minimum of ceremony. *Izakaya* are smaller and more intimate. The menu may change every day, and the sakana is prepared by the master himself. Customers often leave the selection of dishes up to the master or the mama-san, who has an uncanny knack for remembering individual likes and dislikes. Also, the master of an *izakaya* usually serves only his favorite sakés, typically a range from his favorite brewer. For many Japanese, *izakaya* are homes away from home. The casual visitor to an *izakaya* will be greeted with a hearty *Irasshai!* ("Welcome!"), but when a regular comes in, the master, the mama-san, and other regulars may say, *O-kaerinasai!* ("Welcome home!"). This intimacy is by no means exclusive. The welcome extended to newcomers is genuine, and anyone can enjoy the personal touch given to the sakana and the warming of the saké.

Of course, regulars do enjoy certain privileges. The principle of *kamiza* ("highest seat") and *shimoza* ("lowest seat") observed in tatami banquet rooms also applies to the counters and tables of *izakaya*. Customers of long standing automatically take the seats closest to the master, while newer customers take seats closer to the entrance or sit at tables. The interesting thing about this infor-

A long red lantern usually indicates an inexpensive drinking place.

A "mama-san" attends to the food at a typically cramped *izakaya*.

mal etiquette is that it has nothing to do with one's position outside the *izakaya*. Regulars are "drinking friends" (*nomitomodachi*), and it is an unspoken rule at *izakaya* that the realities of status, position, and income that every Japanese must deal with during the day are forgotten.

In this sense, the *noren*, the divided curtains that hang over the entrances of every Japanese-style restaurant or drinking establishment, are much more than substitutes for doors. Passed down from generation to generation, they are objects of great pride among the men and women who make their living in the difficult world that is known as "the water trade." When hung outside a drinking place, they announce that "again tonight we are open." For customers, they are symbols of the separation of the interior of an *izakaya* from the outside world. Here one can relax. Conversations are not about office politics or business deals, but the master's choice of sakana, baseball, or the meaning of life.

All Japanese drinking spots are places for communication. The solitary drinker pouring saké for himself is not a macho image but a sad one. The Japanese usually go out drinking in groups made up of colleagues at work or members of a club, and

the regulars at an *izakaya* form a group based on the place itself.

The lines of communication, however, are quite clearly drawn. One of the unspoken rules of drinking in Japan is that you do not offer to pour saké for someone outside your own party. This rule is one of the most important aspects of the *izakaya* ideal. But it is often disregarded in pubs and bars, where customers are asked to share tables and where the boundaries between groups tend to break down after several tokkuri or bottles of beer. Impromptu conversations can be a wonderful way to make new Japanese friends, but they can also turn out to be unpleasant experiences if someone is too drunk to speak his own language and unable to speak yours. The drunk's habit of imposing himself on other people or other groups is called *karamu* ("wrapping" oneself around another), and it can be as irritating to the Japanese as it will be to you. There is no obligation to tolerate this behavior, and you are well within your rights to spurn such an overture.

Unfortunately, a person too drunk to respect the code may also fail to understand your principled refusal.

Some drinking places carry a large assortment of local sakés.

An *izakaya*'s attractive Japanese interior, with separate tables for small parties.

## The Foreign Saké Drinker in Japan

You may think that the biggest problem facing foreign visitors to Japan is the language. If you are in Japan on business, your hosts will escort you on a tour of Japanese night life, and they will be delighted if you announce that you prefer a *sushi* bar to a steak house, or an *izakaya* to a hostess club. But if you are on your own, the maze of Chinese characters, neon signs, red lanterns, and *noren* curtains in one of the big entertainment districts may make you want to flee back to your hotel, or find a McDonald's. To lose heart, however, is to miss much of the fun of a Japanese evening. All that is really needed is an adventuresome spirit and an observing eye.

The first problem is finding the good places to eat and drink. Most big hotels are located near the great entertainment districts: Akasaka, Ginza, and Shinjuku in Tokyo; Gion and Pontochō in Kyoto; and Minami in Osaka, for example. They can give you information on good places to eat and drink, and "taxi cards" telling your driver how to get to them. Usually, these will be places that cater to foreigners and have menus in English. Keep in mind, however, that hotels tend to recommend places that are in the same price range (expensive) as their own restaurants and bars. Often you can do better setting out on your own, and looking for places is half the fun.

Many Japanese drinking and eating places have glass display cases outside with prices and very convincing plastic models of the dishes on their menus. Other places only display printed menus, and while these are seldom in English, they will give you a good idea of the prices. Often you can figure out the specialty of a place from other signs, or by asking.

Some places have only a small sign with prices for beer, saké, and whiskey, which may or may not reflect prices for food, and others display no prices at all. In such cases, look for other clues. For example, drinking places that display red lanterns, called *akachōchin*, may be pubs that serve a wide variety of dishes or *yakitori* shops, but they are rarely even moderately expensive. Still, many Japanese will

A typical storefront of a *yakitori* shop. Note the row of small lanterns hanging from the eaves. A small placard on the front wall says "Nihonsakari," the name of the saké served here.

not go into a drinking place that does not post prices unless they are introduced by a friend, and you will want to approach them with a good deal of caution, too, especially in large entertainment districts. Eating and drinking in Japan can be unbelievably expensive, and your adventure can take an unpleasant turn if you happen to walk into a high-priced Japanese-style hostess club, or a drinking place that caters to customers with large company expense accounts.

Almost all *izakaya* have large signs advertising the sakés they serve, often provided by the brewer. Try matching the labels on pages 81–84 with the Chinese characters on these signs. Of course, it is easier to ask, or simply take your chances. It is difficult to find places that have a wide range of sakés.

If you are serious about tasting a variety of sakés, or have a particular brand in mind, it is a good idea to start with the *izakaya* recommended on pages 122–24.

Even if the place you finally go into does not have a menu in English, there are still a number of ways you can order the things you want to eat and drink. The first thing to try is ordering in English. All Japanese have to study English in school, so almost everyone speaks some English. If English fails, and the place has a display case, gesture to your waiter to come outside with you, and point to the dishes you want. You can do the same thing with the menus in this book on pages 98–99, which have both Japanese and English for a number of dishes served in most restaurants and drinking places. The word for "please" is *kudasai*. When you point to something on one of these menus say, "*Kore o kudasai*," and you will almost always receive a smile of understanding. You can order in Japanese by simply replacing *kore* with the Japanese name of the dish—*Maguro no sashimi o kudasai*, or *Sake o kudasai*, for example. If you are really daring, try leaving the selection of dishes up to the master or the mama-san (*Sakana wa makasemasu*).

Ordering saké is easy. If you are in an *izakaya* that serves a range of sakés, ask the master if he has your favorite brands—you can point to them in this book. Use the terms we have already mentioned for how you want the sake served—*Hiya*

A popular drinking hole in Yurakuchō, Tokyo, under the tracks of the high-speed Bullet Train. The menu is written on the wall.

An inexpensive outdoor drinking place in the old section of Tokyo's Asakusa, with a brick table, a bottle of white *nigori-zake*, and makeshift benches.

*de kudasai* for room temperature; *Kan o tsukete kudasai* for normal warming; *Nurukan de* for lukewarm; *Rokku de* for on the rocks; and so on.

Unlike bars in the United States, few drinking places in Japan require customers to pay as they go. As in restaurants, you pay as you leave. There are several different pricing systems. In many cheaper pubs and bars, you pay only for what you get. Empty tokkuri and dishes are often left on the table so that a customer can be shown exactly what he has ordered. Since saké is never drunk without sakana, many places serve small plates of food called *o-tōshi* as soon as the customer has been seated. In *izakaya*, these have been selected personally by the master of the shop and should be savored with your first tokkuri while you contemplate what to order. These dishes will usually not appear on your bill, but some places use them as the excuse for a table charge. You may find this annoying, especially if you are served something you don't like, but it does no good whatsoever to refuse this dish (you will be charged for it anyway). A good number of places do not keep any written account of orders at all. The master just makes a rough estimate of how much each customer has had to eat and drink. Almost no eating and drinking establishments in Japan try to cheat customers with this system— they want you to come back. In any case, carefully itemized bills are almost never provided, and charges are rarely questioned.

You may, however, get a receipt, which you can then submit to your employer to be charged off to market research. And this is not at all untrue, for if you really want to know the likes and dislikes of the average Japanese the best time to catch him is when he is safely ensconced in his favorite *izakaya*, safe, warm, and slightly drunk. Following are some typical venues.

## Stand-up Liquor Stores and Yatai

Stand-up liquor stores are one of the least expensive ways of drinking saké in Japan. It is curious that the original "sit-down saké shops" should have been succeeded by liquor stores at which drinkers are obliged to stand at counters, but it is at these unassuming places that the townsman spirit of the old Edo-period *izakaya* still lingers. In most such shops, cup-saké, beer, and small bottles of whiskey are sold at standard retail prices, along with such packaged sakana as dried squid, peanuts, or popcorn. Some actually provide cups for beer or saké, and a few even offer a pan of hot water for warming tokkuri. The clientele of stand-up liquor stores is by no means limited to the impecunious drinker. Like many other traditional shops, these informal places are often centers of neighborhood gossip, great places to just drop in to after a visit to the local public bath.

Only slightly more expensive are *yatai*, portable canopied stalls that appear in the evening near the entrances of major train or subway stations or on street corners in large entertainment districts. *Yatai* vendors specialize in everything from *oden* to *yakitori* to Chinese noodles (*rāmen*), and the sakés they serve range from swill to some really excellent Second Class brews. The main attraction of the *yatai*, however, is the atmosphere. There is nothing like a convivial chat with friends standing around a steaming pot of *oden* and drinking warm saké on a cold winter's evening—especially if you are on your way to a cozy *izakaya*.

Probably the cheapest venue of all is the ubiquitous saké vending machine, which dispenses airplane fuel in warmed glass cups costing about $1 apiece. Very late at night, one sees destitute men or die-hard drinkers huddled around these mechanical bartenders, passing the time in forlorn chatter or waiting for the first train of the morning.

An informal stand-up liquor store, with patrons eating fish out of an open can on the table.

An outdoor drinking stall, or *yatai*, with slatted bamboo screens.

## Yakitori Shops and Oden Shops

*Yakitori* shops, restaurants specializing in grilled chicken on sticks, are among the most popular drinking places in Japan. There are ranks among the places that call themselves *yakitoriya*, with some of them in the *izakaya* class and a great many more in the pub or *nomiya* class. At the bottom are *motsuyakiya*, which serve broiled pork livers, hearts, and tripe instead of chicken. At the top of the scale are well-mannered shops that serve specially bred chicken, and sometimes pheasant, quail, or sparrow, all prepared with great care. *Yakitori* shops can be tiny holes-in-the-wall set up under the railroad tracks near stations or huge pubs that can seat up to 500 customers. The latter often serve a wider variety of food. Whatever form they take, *yakitori* shops are primarily drinking places, and the emphasis is on having fun at minimal expense.

*Oden* shops are similar to *yakitori* shops, but here you encounter a large simmering pot full of various kinds of tofu, fishcakes, dumplings, squid legs, eggs, *daikon* slices, and potatoes. Customers choose what they want from this stew, and it is served with hot mustard. Tako Ume, the famous *oden* restaurant in Osaka's Minami district, includes sliced whale tongue in its *oden*.

Making *yakitori* in a little stall beneath some train tracks in Shibuya, Tokyo. The owner has trained a fan on the grill to spread the delicious fumes of cooking chicken and lure in passersby.

The shop Tako Ume in Osaka, with customers sitting around a luscious *oden* stew. Patrons are drinking out of weighted tin cups.

A *yakitori* shop, fronting on a sidewalk to catch people after work who want a quick one before continuing on their way home.

The well-known Asakusa restaurant Komagata Dōjō. The storefront is built in an old urban townhouse style.

Fanning *unagi* on a large grill.

# Unagi Shops and Dōjō Shops

*Unagi*, or broiled eel, is one of the most savory dishes in the repertoire of Japanese cuisine. It is also considered an excellent health food, and few Japanese will go through the summer without fortifying themselves at least once with a meal of *unagi*. Partly because of its lissome shape, *unagi* is also thought to enhance and preserve feminine beauty. Styles of cooking *unagi* differ in the Tokyo (Kantō) and Kansai regions, but in both areas delicate fillets of *unagi* are broiled lightly over charcoal and basted with a sweet sauce made of soy sauce and saké. Some *unagi* shops also serve eel livers, heads, and crispy deep-fried pieces of eel spine, which are a bit like potato chips. *Unagi* is always served in square Edo-style lacquer trays. Along with *tempura* and *soba* (Japanese noodle) restaurants, *unagi* shops are usually designed in the most beautiful of Japan's old traditional building styles.

If *unagi* is one of Japan's most elegant cuisines, the tiny river eel *dōjō* represents the other end of the scale. There are two ways of serving *dōjō* hotpot style. Traditionally, you began with a sweet broth and threw in handfuls of squirming *dōjō* followed by great quantities of sliced green onions. After adding generous amounts of hot pepper, you crunched away, heads, tails, and all. The style called *Yanagawa nabe* is more popular today. The *dōjō* are cooked with egg and burdock in a special pan that looks like an omelet pan. The shop Komagata Dōjō in Tokyo's Asakusa district is well worth a visit. The owner has re-created the atmosphere of a low-class *nomiya* of the Meiji period, with long wooden planks on a large reed mat and charcoal-burning hibachi. He is also one of the most famous saké connoisseurs in Tokyo, and the rare *jizake* he selects each year for Komagata Dōjō are always an outstanding treat.

*Sushi* can be ordered either one at a time at the counter, or in a set on a tray that one enjoys in a tatami room.

## Sushi Bars

*Sushi* has taken the United States by storm, and there are few Americans who are not familiar with this refined Japanese cuisine. Along with restaurants that specialize in *ike-zukuri*, in which the fish is alive when the chef begins to slice it and is often still moving when served, *sushi* bars are the very best places to eat raw fish. Many Americans, however, like many Japanese, have not mastered the art of enjoying *sushi* while drinking saké. Probably you are most familiar with the style of *sushi* called *nigiri-zushi*, where slices of raw fish are dabbed with a touch of green horseradish (*wasabi*) and pressed onto a cake of vinegared rice. Strictly speaking, however, because saké and rice are not to be consumed together, *nigiri-zushi* should be the last thing you order. The best way to enjoy *sushi* with saké is to order an assortment of *sashimi*, slices of raw fish served in a dish with strands of radish and eaten with soy sauce and horseradish. Even better, order fish or shellfish one at a time, just as you would when ordering *nigiri-zushi* at the counter of a *sushi* bar: freshness is everything when you eat *sashimi*, and the fish will taste better ordered singly than it will if you linger over a large platter. There is no minimum charge at a *sushi* bar. But if you are on a budget, the assorted *sashimi* (*sashimi moriawase*), which has a fixed price, is probably the better deal. Be forewarned that prices are apt to vary from season to season or with availability. And in the best *sushi* bars, where prices are not posted, the tab can easily run to $50 or more per person.

## Fugu Restaurants

*Fugu*, the Japanese globefish, is the rarest of delicacies. Traditionally, it is one of the most dangerous. The ovaries, liver, and some other organs of the fish contain a virulent poison. Today you need not worry, because all restaurants that serve *fugu* are required to employ chefs who have received special training and are licensed by the government. But in the Edo and Meiji periods, *fugu* was one symbol of the connoisseur's willingness to give his life for a single good meal. Even today, older gentlemen speak fondly of the period when you could sample a little of the liver from the *fugu* you had ordered, savoring the numbing sensation caused by the poison. There was an unfortunate accident in 1975 when a famous Kabuki actor died after persuading his chef to serve him a taste of *fugu* liver.

The *torafugu*, or tiger *fugu*, lives only in the waters surrounding Japan and the rivers that empty into them, and it is nearly impossible to obtain this delicacy outside of the country. A full-course *fugu* dinner usually consists of thin slices of the fish and a *fugu* hot-pot. The latter is called *fugu chiri* in Kantō, but *tetchiri* in Kansai (a reference to the *fugu*'s nickname, *teppō*, or "gun"). It is in the finest *fugu* restaurants that one sees dishes in which the delicate, paper-thin slices of fish have been arranged in the pattern of a flower or a Japanese crane. Don't forget to sample *hire-zake*, saké served warm with a *fugu* fin immersed in the cup. Many *fugu* restaurants can be identified by their *fugu* lanterns hanging outside. These are made from genuine *fugu* skins, and show the fish when it has puffed itself up into a round ball.

The restaurant Fukugen in Tsukiji, Tokyo, takes paper-thin strips of *fugu* and arranges them into the shape of a chrysanthemum flower.

# Ryōtei

*Ryōtei* are the 20th-century successors of the elegant tea houses of the Edo period, and it is here that you may be entertained by geisha in the traditional Japanese style. *Ryōtei* symbolize Japanese connoisseurship at its most highly developed and, along with the geisha, are rapidly declining in numbers. Few Japanese are completely comfortable in the realm of the *ryōtei*, which demands an exhaustive knowledge of traditional Japanese arts and etiquette.

While the emphasis is on pleasure, the world of a Japanese *ryōtei* is essentially that of the ceremonial tea room. Many *ryōtei* also specialize in *kaiseki*, the multi-dished cuisine of the tea ceremony. But there is no need for you to feel constrained; the basic outline of etiquette at formal banquets in this book, plus a few additional pointers, will get you through a meal at any *ryōtei*.

Geisha are not always invited to parties at *ryōtei*, but if they are, you will want to know how to deal with them (a surprising number of geisha speak a fair amount of English). Important to remember is that geisha do not appreciate comments on their appearance. Geisha take great pride in the fact that they are selling their art and not their bodies, and no matter how well intentioned, comments on their desirability as sexual objects are out of place. For the same reason, it is rude to talk with other people when geisha are performing. Conversations should be saved for lapses in the entertainment, when the geisha are busy doing *o-shaku* for guests.

Having a meal at a *ryōtei* is one of the best ways to understand traditional Japanese concepts of elegance. Take your time and observe everything. While the places we have mentioned so far are usually shops in larger buildings, the *ryōtei* is typically a rambling Japanese-style house, with everything immaculately designed and laid out from the entryway all along the corridors that lead to your private banquet room. Some of the finest private gardens in Japan are to be found in *ryōtei*—not to mention priceless collections of pottery and artwork. Foods served during the meal will be beautifully arranged on a variety of plates and trays that have been selected with scrupulous attention to the season and the way they harmonize with the food and the other items in the room. Similar care will be lavished on the flower arrangement in the ceremonial alcove of your room.

Needless to say, *ryōtei* can be extremely exclusive. Some *ryōtei* will not accept new customers unless they have been introduced by a regular guest. Reservations are always essential, usually well in advance.

Minokō is a *ryōtei* in Kyoto, serving *kaiseki* and other Kyoto-style foods. The stone pathway leading from the gate to the main entryway passes through a small Japanese garden.

If you want to go to a *ryōtei* in Kyoto's Gion district, for example, you should have your travel agent make reservations at one of the *ryōtei* that caters to foreigners at the same time that he books your hotel. Of course, *ryōtei* are not cheap. Dinner will cost $150 and up, and if you are attended by geisha the bill will be about twice that. The best way of enjoying the atmosphere of a *ryōtei* without spending a great deal of money is to make a reservation for a luncheon there. This will be prepared with all the care given to an evening banquet, and will cost you from $40 to $100—a bargain.

# 40 Izakaya: A Selection

The Japanese drinking places listed on this page and the following two pages are recommended here because they offer you a chance to sample a range of good sakés and provide something—cuisine, atmosphere, courtesy—that will give you a taste of the rich world of Japanese connoisseurship. The list is by no means exhaustive—in almost every Japanese neighborhood you will find at least one upstanding establishment that caters to a knowledgeable and selective clientele.

Reservations and credit cards are often not accepted at smaller *izakaya*, and you are advised not to go in a large group, as these places are intimate and seating may be limited. Loud talk and boisterous behavior are for the same reason unacceptable—no table hopping, please, and remember that these are not singles bars or collegetown pubs. The nearest train or subway station appears in parentheses after the address.

---

TOKYO

**BOTAN**          03-232-9508

Sankō Bldg., Takadanobaba 1-25-29, Shinjuku-ku, Tokyo 160 (TAKADANO-BABA)

Moderate. 17:00–23:00. Closed Sundays, holidays.

Quiet and informal, very clean and friendly. Serves over thirty-five *jizake*. Will keep unfinished bottles until your next visit.

**CHIRIMBŌ**          03-350-6945

Shinjuku 3-8-7, Shinjuku-ku, Tokyo 160 (SHINJUKU 3-CHŌME)

Inexpensive. 17:00–5:00. Closed Sundays.

*Yatai*-style country inn interior, with separate booths. Very popular with young people.

**DAITOKAI**          03-981-6617

Minami Ikebukuro 1-19-10, Toshima-ku, Tokyo 171 (IKEBUKURO)

Inexpensive. 17:00–7:00. Open every day.

Very large with tatami rooms and sunken hearths. Popular with young people. Big selection of sakana.

**EDO ICHI**          03-945-3032

Minami Ōtsuka 2-45-4, Toshima-ku, Tokyo 170 (ŌTSUKA)

Moderate. 17:00–22:00. Closed Sundays, holidays.

Seating around cypress counter. Good selection of *jizake*. Fresh, inexpensive sakana.

**HACHIMAKI OKADA**          03-561-0357

Ginza 3-7-21, Chūō-ku, Tokyo 104 (GINZA 1-CHŌME)

Expensive. 16:30–21:00. Closed Sundays, holidays.

Serves Kiku-Masamune *taru-zake*. Specializes in Kantō-style (Tokyo) cuisine.

**HANTEI**          03-828-1440

Nezu 2-12-15, Bunkyō-ku, Tokyo 113 (NEZU)

Moderate. 17:00–23:00. Closed Mondays.

Lovely three-story wooden building in one of Tokyo's older sections. Serves sakés from Hiroshima. Specializes in over two dozen kinds of *kushi-age*: deep-fried meats and vegetables on skewers.

**ICHI NO CHAYA**          03-251-8517

Kanda Awaji-chō 2-21-10, Chiyoda-ku, Tokyo 101 (KANDA)

Moderate. 17:00–23:00. Closed Sundays, holidays.

Folkcraft-style interior. Offers twenty different *jizake*.

**ISETŌ**          03-260-6363

Kagurazaka 4-2, Shinjuku-ku, Tokyo 162 (KAGURAZAKA)

Moderate. 17:00–21:00. Closed Sundays, holidays.

Old-style atmosphere with sakés warmed over charcoal. Offers a set course of sakana.

**IWATEYA**          03-831-9317

Yushima 3-38-8, Bunkyō-ku, Tokyo 113 (UENO)

Inexpensive. 16:00–22:00. Closed Sundays, holidays.

Family-style place popular with University of Tokyo professors. Specializes in cuisine from Iwate Prefecture. Serves Suishin saké.

**KURA**          03-986-3926

Nishi Ikebukuro 1-28-1, Toshima-ku, Tokyo 171 (IKEBUKURO)

Moderate. 11:30–23:00. Open every day.

Seasonal specialities and fourteen kinds of *jizake* in a basement designed to resemble a samurai household.

**KUREMUTSU**          03-842-0906

Asakusa 2-2, Taitō-ku, Tokyo 111 (ASAKUSA)

Moderate. 16:00–22:00. Closed Thursdays.

Distinctive atmosphere. Specializes in Japanese-style cooking, but no *tempura* or *unagi*. Raw seafood and deep-fried tofu are good. Saké is Kembishi.

**MASUMOTO**          03-501-9820

Toranomon 1-8-16, Minato-ku, Tokyo 105 (TORANOMON)

Inexpensive. 16:00–21:30. Closed Sundays, holidays.

Stopping-off place for government workers on their way home. Seating at long banquet tables. Famous for its octopus *oden*.

**MATSUKAZE** 03-841-0020

Asakusa 1-15-6, Taitō-ku, Tokyo 111 (ASAKUSA)

Inexpensive. 16:00–22:00. Closed Tuesdays.

Offers array of fine sakés in small quarters near famous temple in the old city. Limit of three tokkuri to the customer.

**MATSURI BAYASHI** 03-464-5297

Katei Bldg., Udagawa-chō 31-9, Shibuya-ku, Tokyo 150 (SHIBUYA)

Moderate. 15:00–2:00. Closed third Monday of each month.

Has about sixty *jizake* on hand. No beer or whiskey—just saké.

**MISATO** 03-985-6379

Higashi Ikebukuro 1-31-6, Toshima-ku, Tokyo 170 (IKEBUKURO)

Moderate. 17:00–24:00. Closed Sundays, holidays.

Seating at long tables. One hundred varieties of *jizake*. Famous for its homemade cuisine.

**NEBOKE** 03-585-9640

Akasaka 3-11-17, Minato-ku, Tokyo 107 (AKASAKA MITSUKE)

Expensive. 11:30–22:30. Closed Sundays, holidays.

Specializes in Tosa cuisine from Shikoku, especially bonito *sashimi*. Serves Tsukasabotan saké.

**NEZU NO JIMPACHI** 03-823-1309

Nezu 2-26-4, Bunkyō-ku, Tokyo 113 (NEZU)

Moderate. 17:00–21:00. Closed Sundays.

Famous old-fashioned *izakaya* with rope *noren* curtain. Popular with connoisseurs from all over Tokyo who come to sample the sakana and the master's selection of fine sakés.

**NOMBEI DŌJŌ** 03-784-3871

Nakanobu 5-11-19, Shinagawa-ku, Tokyo 142 (EBARACHŌ)

Moderate. 17:00–23:00. Closed Sundays.

Selected *jizake* from around Japan. Very good *sashimi*.

**OKAJŌKI** 03-388-3753

Nakano 5-59-3, Nakano-ku, Tokyo 164 (NAKANO)

Inexpensive. 17:00–23:00. Open every day.

Good cuisine from Aomori Prefecture, especially grilled fish.

**SAKABAYASHI HANNA** 03-405-9888

Minami Aoyama 1-25-2, Minato-ku, Tokyo 107 (NOGIZAKA)

Inexpensive. 17:00–23:00. Closed Sundays, holidays.

Offers *jizake* from all over Japan. Only small tidbits for sakana, but very good.

**SAKE NO ANA** 03-567-1131

Ginza 3-5-8, Chūō-ku, Tokyo 104 (GINZA)

Moderate. 11:30–22:00. Closed New Year's Day.

Seventy-six kinds of *jizake*, served full-measure. You warm the tokkuri yourself at the table.

**SASASHU** 03-971-6796

Ikebukuro 2-2-2, Toshima-ku, Tokyo 171 (IKEBUKURO)

Moderate. 17:00–22:00. Closed Sundays, holidays.

Forty different fine sakés personally selected by the master. A favorite with connoisseurs.

**SASAYA** 03-561-5037

Kyōbashi 2-10-1, Chūō-ku, Tokyo 104 (KYŌBASHI)

Moderate. 17:00–22:00. Closed Saturdays, Sundays, holidays.

Popular with office workers. Simple country-style cuisine.

**SHINSUKE** 03-832-0469

Yushima 3-31-5, Bunkyō-ku, Tokyo 113 (UENO)

Moderate. 17:00–22:00. Closed Sundays, holidays.

Interior resembles Taishō-period *nomiya*. Popular with University of Tokyo professors and their students.

**TARUMATSU** 03-834-1363

Ueno 6-4-13, Taitō-ku, Tokyo 110 (UENO)

Inexpensive. 16:00–23:00. Open every day.

Serves only *taru-zake* from large casks. Many kinds of sakana, all very good.

**TENGU** 03-349-0858

Nishiguchi Kaikan, Nishi Shinjuku 1-1-1, Shinjuku-ku, Tokyo 160 (SHINJUKU)

Inexpensive. 17:00–23:30. Open every day.

Cavernous drinking hall that seats 500. Offers fourteen *jizake*, including Aramasa served chilled. Popular with young people.

KYOTO

### HANAFUSA 075-211-8874

Shijō Agaru Uradera Dōri, Nakano-chō, Nakagyō-ku, Kyoto 604 (SHIJŌ KAWARAMACHI)

Expensive. 17:00–23:00. Closed Thursdays.

Family-style cuisine. Very cozy, with seats for twenty people. Serves Hakushika saké.

### KIKŌ 075-351-7856

Futatsujime Higashi Iru Kitagawa, Shijō Kawaramachi Kudaru, Shimogyō-ku, Kyoto 604 (KAWARAMACHI)

Moderate. 17:00–23:00. Closed Mondays.

All saké personally selected by the master. Simmering tofu (*yudōfu*) especially good.

### TOTOSHIN 075-711-3759

Deguchi-machi 17-7, Ichijōji, Sakyō-ku, Kyoto 606 (ICHIJŌ)

Moderate. 17:00–22:00. Closed Mondays.

Specializes in Kyoto-style *sushi*. Good range of *jizake*.

### YAMATOMI 075-221-1364

Nabeyamachi Shijō Agaru, Pontochō, Nakagyō-ku, Kyoto 604 (SHIJŌ)

Inexpensive. 12:00–24:00. Closed Wednesdays.

Good for saké and meals. Suitable for families. In summer you can sit overlooking the banks of the Kamo River.

OSAKA

### GIMPEI 06-341-6000

Dōjima 1-5-4, Kita-ku, Osaka 530 (NISHI UMEDA)

Expensive. 17:00–24:00. Closed Sundays, holidays.

Excellent *sashimi*. Choose your own live fish from the tank. Serves Ozeki saké.

### HONJIN 06-312-3751

Sonezaki 2-10-18, Kita-ku, Osaka 530 (UMEDA)

Expensive. 16:00–4:00. Open every day.

Done up in the style of an Edo-period inn reserved for feudal lords and other important personages. Family-style cooking.

### ICHIFUJI 06-345-8367

Sonezaki Shinchi 1-1-15, Kita-ku, Osaka 530 (YODOYABASHI)

Expensive. 11:30–22:00. Closed Sundays, holidays.

Specializes in grilled foods on skewers. Serves Ozeki saké.

### KAKASHI 06-312-9177

Togano-chō 15-3, Kita-ku, Osaka 530 (UMEDA)

Expensive. 16:30–5:00. Open every day.

Country-style cooking. Select your own live fish from the tank. Good selection of *jizake*.

### MUTEKIRŌ 06-314-3232

Sonezaki 2-13-4, Kitaku, Osaka 530 (UMEDA)

Expensive. 17:00–2:00. Open every day.

Interior re-creates the building style of the Meiji period. Specializes in tofu and fish.

### TŌFUYA 06-211-9017

Namba 1-5-6, Minami-ku, Osaka 542 (NAMBA)

Moderate. 17:00–23:00. Closed Sundays, holidays.

As the name implies, the specialty is tofu, prepared in a variety of different styles.

KOBE

### NOMBE KAMADO 078-391-8681

Kotobuki Sannomiya Bldg., Kita Nagasa Dōri 1-9-1, Chūō-ku, Kobe 651 (SANNOMIYA)

Inexpensive. 17:00–23:30. Open every day.

Interior re-creates a drinking house of the Edo period. Sakana are prepared in an old-style kilnlike oven.

### OKAGAWA 078-222-3511

Kitano-chō 1-5-10, Chūō-ku, Kobe 650 (SANNOMIYA)

Moderate. 11:00–22:00. Open every day.

A *tempura* shop. Serves only Hakutsuru saké.

### TORIMITSU 078-731-5855

Miyuki-chō 1-39, Suma-ku, Kobe 654 (SUMA)

Moderate. 11:30–22:00. Closed Mondays.

Great *yakitori*. Folkcraft-style interior.

### YAMAGATAYA YASUHISA 078-452-2905

Motoyama Kita-machi 11-7, Higashi Nada-ku, Kobe 658 (OKAMOTO)

Moderate. 17:00–22:00. Closed Mondays.

Fine collection of porcelain. Serves *yakitori* and other fowl.

# Saké Distributors in the United States

The following firms are all currently distributing saké in the United States: the brands they carry appear here in small capital letters and include imported as well as U.S.–made sakés. The main sales outlets are liquor stores, Japanese restaurants, and Oriental groceries. For further information contact the distributors or consult your local telephone directory.

**CAPITOL DISTRIBUTORS**
55–60 58th Street
Maspeth, NY 11378
(212) 326-3000
GENJI, CHIYODA

**CHARMER INDUSTRIES**
19–50 48th Street
Astoria, NY 11105
(212) 726-2500
CHIYODA, GENJI, GEKKEIKAN

**GENERAL LIQUOR**
12017 Mack Avenue
Detroit, MI 48215
(313) 823-5566
ICHIDAI

**JASON BROOKE IMPORTS**
380 North Broadway
Jericho, NY 11753
(516) 822-8586
SAWANOTSURU

**HEUBLEIN**
16 Munson Road
Farmington, CT 06032
(800) 243-5110
KIKU-MASAMUNE

**JFC INTERNATIONAL**
4353 Exchange Avenue
Los Angeles, CA 90058
(213) 587-3900
MEIMONSHUKAI BRANDS (THROUGH RESTAURANT NIPPON), OZEKI (USA)

**K AND M IMPORT**
515 Maynard Avenue South
Seattle, WA 98104
(206) 622-8874
HAKUSHIKA, NIHONSAKARI, OZEKI (USA), SHIRAYUKI, SHO CHIKU BAI (USA), TAKARA MASAMUNE (USA)

**KNICKERBOCKER LIQUORS**
99 Lafayette Drive
Syosset, NY 11791
(800) 632-4411
ICHIDAI

**LONE STAR**
P.O. Box 3228
Houston, TX 77253
(713) 928-5721
CHIYODA

**MONSIEUR HENRI WINES**
707 Westchester Avenue
White Plains, NY 10604
(914) 997-0100
FU-KI

**MUTUAL TRADING**
431 Crocker Street
Los Angeles, CA 90013
(213) 626-9458
HAKU-TAKA, KAMOTSURU, SHO CHIKU BAI (USA), TAKARA MASAMUNE (USA)

**NISHIMOTO TRADING**
410 East Grand Avenue
South San Francisco, CA 94080
(415) 871-2490
HAKUTSURU, OZEKI (USA), SAWANOTSURU, SHO CHIKU BAI (USA), TAKARA MASAMUNE (USA)

**NOR-GLO IMPORT**
3060 Pharr Court N., N.W.
Atlanta, GA 30305
(404) 233-4789
FUJU

**NORTH AMERICAN FOOD**
412 R Street
Sacramento, CA 95814
(916) 442-0618
SHO CHIKU BAI (USA)

**PARADISE BEVERAGES**
2850 Paa Street
Honolulu, HI 96819
(808) 833-3044
TAKARA MASAMUNE

**PEERLESS IMPORTERS**
16 Bridgewater Street
Brooklyn, NY 11222
(212) 389-7900
CHIYODA, FU-KI, GEKKEIKAN, GENJI, SHOGUN

**SCHENLEY INDUSTRIES**
888 7th Avenue
New York, NY 10019
(212) 621-8000
HAKUTSURU

**SIDNEY FRANK IMPORTING**
770 Lexington Avenue
New York, NY 10021
(212) 371-1447
GEKKEIKAN

**SOUTHERN WINE**
1600 NW 163rd Street
Miami, FL 33169
(305) 625-4171
GEKKEIKAN

**SOUTHERN WINE AND SPIRITS OF CALIFORNIA**
17101 Valley View Avenue
Cerritos, CA 90701
(213) 926-2000
SHO CHIKU BAI (USA)

**UNION LIQUOR**
3247 South Kedzie
Chicago, IL 60623
(312) 254-9000
ICHIDAI, KAMITAKA

**WILLIAM GRANT AND SONS**
130 Fieldcrest Avenue
Edison, NJ 08837
(201) 225-9000
GENJI

**WINE OF JAPAN IMPORTER**
21–59 Broad Avenue
Long Island City, NY 11101
(212) 729-2876
SHIRAYUKI, TAKARA MASAMUNE (USA)

125

# Index

# Acknowledgments

The original Japanese text for *Saké A Drinker's Guide* was translated and adapted into English by Mark A. Harbison. The Publisher herein wishes to express its gratitude to the many organizations, institutions, and individuals that contributed to the planning and production of this book, especially Kaoru Furukawa; the Izumiya Liquor Store of Kanda, Tokyo, and its owners, Mr. and Mrs. Tatsuyuki Yokota, for introducing the editors to many fine sakés and to the true meaning of connoisseurship; the Japan Saké Brewers Association, for information and assistance; Kidoizumi Shuzō, makers of Kidoizumi saké; Masanobu Kitani; Maruhachi, of Nezu, its staff, and its owners, Takashi and Chiyae Inō; Nihon Meimonshukai (Okanage Co., Ltd.); Kikuo Noshiro, Professor, Tokyo University of Agriculture; Ogimura Shikki-ten, for supplying the *toso* set on page 55; Restaurant Nippon, of New York City; Shiambashi, of Shintomi-chō, Tokyo, for supplying the venue for the back-jacket photograph, and Miss June Kahler, who modeled for it; Shibata Shoten, publishers of *Izakaya* magazine; Tokiko Suzuki, for the sakana recipes on pages 104-5 and the two hot-pots on pages 108-9; Tarumatsu, of Ueno, Tokyo, for some memorable evenings; Utsunomiya Shuzō, makers of Shikizakura saké.

Among the companies, photographers, and illustrators who provided visual material for this book are Asahi Shinbun Photo Service, page 53; Dandi Photo, page 34 (bottom); Kunio Ekiguchi, pages 98-99; Hiroshi Hamaya, page 10 (bottom); Seiichi Hayashi, title pages; Jun Ichiura, page 88 (bottom); Hiromichi Inoue, pages 10 (top), 38 (left), 39, 40 (bottom), 49 (right), 52, 74 (bottom); Takashi Kakinuma, page 95 (bottom); Keizō Kaneko, pages 25 (bottom), 33, 40 (top), 55 (top, bottom), 60, 62 (bottom), 73, 74 (top), 75, 80 (top center), 93 (top), 110 (top left), 116, 119 (top); Michio Kojima, endpapers; Kyoto National Museum, pages 11 (bottom), 58-59 (top); Tadashi Masuda, pages 110 (top right, bottom), 111 (top left, bottom right); Meiji Kinenkan, page 55 (center); Hiroshi Mizobuchi, pages 58 (bottom left), 92 (top); Manabu Oda, page 120 (bottom); Yoshikatsu Saeki, pages 106, 107 (bottom); Hiroji Seki, pages 13, 42, 45, 50-51, 72, 91 (center), 92 (bottom), 93 (bottom), 94, 95 (top), 96; Hiroto Sensui, pages 25 (center), 27 (top), 28 (top), 29, 31 (left), 32, 62 (center), 71, 91 (top and bottom), 112, 114-15, 117, 118 (top, bottom left), 120 (bottom); Makoto Shimomura, page 107 (top); Kiyoshi Takai, pages 35, 110 (center left), 111 (top right, bottom left); Tankei Library, page 34 (top); Akihiko Tokue, pages 54, 64, 98-99; Shinzō Uchida, page 14; Tōyō Yamamoto, page 59 (bottom left, right); Chiaki Yoshida, page 58 (center); Manabu Yunoki, pages 30, 38 (right); Yūzankaku Shuppan, pages 76-78.

The Publisher wishes to thank the following for generously allowing reproduction of objects in their collections: Gotō Art Museum, for *Murasaki Shikibu Nikki Ekotoba*, page 11; Isonokami Shrine, for the saké vat, page 10; Hajimu Kaneda, for *Shunjū Shijo Yūraku-zu*, page 22; Nagasaki Municipal Museum, for *Kagetsu Ranjin Yūkyō-zu*, page 12; National Diet Library, for the illustration from *Agura-nabe*, page 28; National Museum of Japanese History, for the scene of Hideyoshi's cherry-blossom-viewing party *(Daigo Hanami-zu Byōbu)*, page 23; Sanjichion-ji, for *Shuhan-ron*, page 11; Tōdaiji, for the statue of Kongō Rikishi, page 18; Tokugawa Reimeikai Foundation, for the lacquerware stand, page 20; Tokyo National Museum, for *Kinsei Shokunin-zukushi Ekotoba*, page 12, and for *Kabuki-zu Byōbu*, pages 56-57; Tokyo University of Agriculture, Museum of Brewing, for the saké utensils on page 25, for the scene of an Edo-period drinking establishment *(Izakaya Fūkei)* on page 27, for the Utagawa print *(Suirō Yūen-zu)* on page 28, for the Issen print on page 29, for the wartime utensils on page 31, for the gourd-container and *tsunodaru* on page 62, and for the saké warmers on page 91; Takashi Yanagi, for *Yūraku-zu Byōbu*, pages 12 and 20-21.

Acknowledgment is also made to the following books and publishers that were valuable sources of visual material and information: *Gensen Nihon no Aji* (Kodansha, 1982), for the photograph of Fukugen, page 120; *Hitorigurashi: Sake to Sakana* (Kodansha, 1981), for the photographs on pages 102-3 and recipes; *Nada no Sake Hakubutsukan* (Kodansha, 1983); *Nihon no Meiryōtei* (Japan Travel Bureau, 1983), for the photograph of Oimatsu, page 95; *Nihon no Meishu Jiten* (Kodansha, 1978), for the photographs on pages 1, 9, 15, 26 (top and bottom), 36, 49 (left), 61, 62 (top), 63, 100-1, 111 (center left), 123; *Nihonshu* (Mainichi Shinbunsha, 1983), for the photographs of Ai Kanzaki and Kyōkei Ōmoto, page 59; *Nihonshu no Kenkyū* (Chūō Kōron-sha, 1981); *Otoko no Teryōri, Ore no Sakana* (Kodansha, 1980), for the photograph of simmering tofu, page 107; *Seikatsubunkashi* (Yūzankaku Shuppan, 1984), for the illustrations on pages 76-78; *Shūkan Asahi Hyakka: Sake*, no. 111 (Asahi Shinbunsha, 1983); *Wakai Josei* (Kodansha, 1979), for the photographs of hot-pots, pages 106-7. The Saikaku quotation on page 26 is from *Some Final Words of Advice*, translated by Peter Nosco (Charles E. Tuttle, 1980, page 44). The Venables quotation on page 30 is from *Behind the Smile in Real Japan* (George G. Harrap, 1936, pages 92-93). The verse from the "Grinding the Moto" song on page 44 was cited in *Nihon no Sake*, by Kin'ichirō Sakaguchi (Iwanami Shinsho, 1964, pages 132-33).

TELL US WHAT YOU THINK

The Publisher welcomes comments from readers about their reactions to this book, their favorite sakés and drinking establishments, and any aspects of drinking and eating Japanese style that they would like to know more about. Please address all correspondence to The Editor, *Saké: A Drinker's Guide*, Kodansha International, 12-21, Otowa 2-chome, Bunkyo-ku, Tokyo 112, Japan.

定価2,900円
in Japan